Brexit: The Isolated Island

Norman B. Lechat

A product of Pouncing Panda Productions

Published by Pouncing Panda Productions®

Pouncing Panda Productions is part of LEG holdings® and are both registered trademarks having their offices in the complex of:

LEG, 5 rue Caspard Mathias Spoo, Luxembourg, L-2546

Author photo courtesy of Jean Grotz, *GRT* Sàrl

Cover design is and remains property of Christophe Lima, *Free Spirit* Sàrl

Printed by CreateSpace

ISBN:1533354162
ISBN-13: 978-1533354167

DEDICATION

I dedicate this to the sickness which left me bed ridden and unable to work for so much of the last year. I am therefore grateful to all those who helped during this time so that this book, albeit one year later than planned can actually be released in time for Britain's most important date of the 21st century.

CONTENTS

PREFACE

"To be or not to be…"

Baird William's poignant prose sums up excellently the referendum question, and is thus a typically English way to visit one of her historical moments. But this is not a Shakespeare tragedy, or at least not until the decision goes wrong.

Britain, these islands isolated geographically from mainland Europe; once she was Great, however just one referendum and she can be anything but. Vote to stay, vote to leave, there should be no fighting on the beaches, but there could be happy flag wave or two from the white cliffs of Dover as this group of islands drift off into sunset, and to the rest of our lives.

It may no longer have a cigar wielding gentleman, nor an iron lady, preparing for the worst but hoping for the best type. This alone could be the tragedy, but time may prove Britain's unrequited love with weak-willed leaders is over and rule Britannia can be sung once again with pride, or, could it be the whistle of Beethoven's Ode to joy.

But for now it is the turn of the people. Britain, now more than ever needs to be a kingdom united. Whatever the outcome, the government needs to act like a coalition of all the sensible sides. Does Britain push itself off from the coast of France, or throw out the tie ropes and be pulled closer? Pick your team, and see if you change allegiances as we discover together where it will get us.

Brexit (adj.) Historical term used to describe the possibility of the exit from Europe of the small but Great Britain... For the future definition, please read on.

1 BREXIT: BRITAIN GREAT ONCE AGAIN

"Wisdom is oftentimes nearer when we stoop than when we soar" - Wordsworth

Grexit, a term accredited as coming from Citigroup's Buiter and Rahbari. As media does, a cheap pun recycled and Brexit occupies the headlines. A quick search on Google for this term and over 39 million results are proposed. Is it really a big deal, or is there just a lack of news at the moment? After all, it is but a cluster of specks on a map. An island no one dreams of as an exotic location. Sun trap is not it's keyword, her beaches are far from golden, and her few palm trees suffer from the chills. So for those who will pick up this book in twenty years and see what Europe used to be, here is a recap of the other headlines:

We have the potential of World War Three close by. Russia doing fly-bys on American military ships, Russia retaliating to being shot down by a country which is apparently an ally (do not worry Russia, friends often come in strange packages…). China and South Korea having ongoing concerns with a funny haircut wielding small time dictator (because Amazon and global internet are banned in his country I can write this knowing he will not be reading it anytime soon).

A movement of plain evil is culling people in their thousands in the middle and near east. There are cold genocides on holiday beaches and in capital cities. The Arab spring is still not settled, Boko Haram runs riot after claiming media attention almost five years ago, and famine is no better now than Egypt circa Joseph, yet food can be traded as a financial product. Just for good measure let's throw in the latest spate of lone shooters in America. If the four Horsemen of the apocalypse rode the earth now, they would be happy with their progress.

Then for the financial side; panic from the Chinese economic slowdown has echoed through markets, twice. This was helped only by OPEC's desire to drive out competition in the Oil Market, which worked well - their members such as Venezuela will testify to that. And to top it all off, a potential American president said something inappropriate during a presidential campaign (one is welcome to read this as 'many things'). Although none quite yet as bad as the 26th June 1963 "Ich bin ein Berliner"... fifty four years later and we still laugh - thanks Kennedy. Or maybe it was a prophetic message that future President Trump is the pastry...

What a piece of work is man! And a bundle of joy the global economy! As an investor in global markets, this is play time, but as a human made up of feelings and sentiments, it is also a sad time.

Britain has the chance to stand up and be counted; to pay attention to now so as to influence the future. The polls are close, the votes and valuable, the outcome not a foregone conclusion. Does the country that has flirted, fought for and against Europe throughout centuries finally settle down and go the whole way, or does it turn its back on the Union with Europe? It is so easy today to find an escape from all the negativity. We switch the TV channels, we load a different internet page, we 'like' pointless things that keep us away from standing up for what matters. Intent to avoid problems, we sometimes aimlessly wander out of the frying pan. And those that have wandered that way before can testify and stand witness that it can be a hotter landing than one anticipates.

2 EUROPE! BUT WHO ARE YOU?

"Friends, Romans, countrymen, lend me your ears" – Shakespeare

Rome was the location for this speech opener of Marc Antony in Julius Caesar, and it is one with an undertone ploy to get people on his side. Europe to a Brit, or at least to many an Englishman has that same feel. Britain has a disconnection with Europe, but I am yet to find a consistent answer as to why that is. I myself, I have no good answer even from my own point of view. 'Should Britain be a part of it' seems like the sort of question one can shrug his shoulders to, as if no precise answer can allow a nonchalant response. The computer game 'Lemmings' took my generation by storm. Small animals that marched and chanted in whatever direction the lead lemming went. Certain lemmings had tasks such as building bridges to avoid that they all mindlessly walking off a cliff. Europe, presents opportunities to Britain, and vice versa. But, is it a bridge of safety, or a cliff of uncertain death? One should understand the very existence of Europe and where it is aims to go.

It essentially started due to repeated conflicts. The second half of the Industrial Revolution was finishing across several countries, and it was becoming a 'my dad is bigger than your dad' challenge between a handful of countries located in close proximity. The Great War commenced. Three years later and many lives needlessly lost; the war came to a truce. One generation later and an Austrian decided his adopted father Germany was the biggest dad at the School Fun Run.

His desire to rule could not be checked by other countries' leaders, who readied themselves to help Poland, a country in need. Ignored pleas for peace turned into the ultimatum being passed from Britain's ambassador to Germany, then at 11.15 on the 3rd September 1939, the war that changed the world began. Economies crashed, countries were devastated, and much worse; many lives taken. The population control via the War system is a cruel one.

Two Wars in thirty years brought doomsayers to the fore in questioning if this was the end of the world. Well it could have been Jim, but not as they knew it. Countries situated on the European continent knew however that something needed to change for lasting peace. America - nowadays known and loved for their Fast Food - was eager to show the world that they were no longer just a land of pilgrims, cowboys and Indians fighting to get out of the 'oppressive shadow of the meddling English'; they demonstrated to the world their love of over-sizing everything with the original Big Mac; The Hydrogen Bomb.

With these two colossal wars over and peace needing to be brought to opposing countries, a long road was ahead. The memory of war still remains strong on people's minds, even generations later; proof of this is found on Spanish holiday islands every time a German lays down a towel upon a Sun Lounger. Forgive and forget is no easy task. Circa 1950 and the solutions to the problems were on the horizon if one vital question aimed at bringing peace and growth could be answered:
How can mercy be extended to a country whose aim was world domination?

Easy. Love your enemies; do well to them and help them grow... That is indeed exactly what happened and the result was amazing; Germany, a testimony to what can happen when countries work together has grown to one of the most stable countries in the world. One to which the world looks for mechanical and engineering reliability. (Note to Adolf; This, Adolf, is the only true way to show you have the best dad.)

Financial support from across the Atlantic came into Europe, or at least Western Europe long before these countries even got on their feet and around a table. The results have been outstanding. 66 years later and many economic and political agreements are in place, working and most importantly; no more wars amongst the partaking countries.

This financial support of the late 1940's came in the shape of the Marshall Plan in an attempt to stop communism. This funding of 'Western Europe' was aimed at rebuilding economies and stopping the advancement of Communism spreading into Eastern Europe.

The money and ideas which flowed into this plan led mainly to the rebuilding of European industry, knowing that this is the chief economic growth factor to the beneficiary countries. This influx split geographical Europe, to a point into two real groups; Western Europe, and the rest. Britain, actually was the cat which got the cream, receiving over 20 per cent of the funding which came through the plan. As with any growing economy, progress would actually need to come from within and even though Britain was doing well for itself, it was a handful of the continental countries which moved to the next step of the unity which was to develop over the coming generations.

Robert Schuman presented his declaration to unite several European countries via the pooling of steel and coal. France, West Germany, Italy and the trio of Benelux came together and that was the start of Europe; the European Coal and Steel Community.

The French Foreign Minister appeared to have done more than just a declaration, instead he performed a Schumann Special worthy of the Hollywood film 'Oceans Twelve'. In the film, the group of 'opportunists' lifted a house in Amsterdam to make possible a theft of the first stock market certificate. What the political Schuman did was actually raise several economies based on the industrial strength of Germany and the resources at its disposal. Interesting then, that the French President Charles De Gaulle did not want the help that Britain could bring, and thus he vetoed their application to join the ECSC. Statistics of the time showed that De Gaulle and the French economy in particular were not exactly the hardest worker in this group of nations.

France not only produced less steel, but also took longer in doing so than their ECSC counterparts; in fact, France had an inefficiency factor of up to 50 per cent on Germany and Italy, and as a result ended up keeping their own supplies for a later period. All the while, it allowed for a discounting from German and Italian steel – ironic or clever? You can decide.

These two efficient nations chose quite different routes for their economic progress; Germany let the material producers get on with it, while Italy invested heavily through subsidies allowing the improvement of technology. To think, Italy was once a forerunner in Europe, and is now one of the worst ten performers in terms of GDP growth. How times have changed, and a lesson taught that leading the way is not always the best idea.

Those who are of an earlier generation in life will remember there was a dream. The dream was not that of Martin Luther King, it was not even a John Lennon song of hope, but was the brainchild of the afore-mentioned French Foreign Minister Robert Schuman.
"Europe will not be made all at once, or according to a single plan. It will be built through concrete achievements which first create a *de facto* solidarity."

Together, Europe should grow together and become a superpower. One that could match America and the Soviet Union. The Marshall Plan helped these economies get back on their feet and has seen this aided project develop nicely.

Ironically, Russia and America; eventual allies against the Nazi ideology have since turned into potential enemies. Many songs have been sung about the relationship between these two geographical behemoths which comprise the bread of the Europe sandwich. Sting reminds us of the Soviet Union taunts in the 1985 hit 'Russians'. Bob Dylan summarises the mentality with which Americans were brought up when he penned "I've learned to hate the Russians". The cold war diffused, yet the only heat shared between these countries isn't a gentle fuzzy warming around the same living room fire, but that of the edginess with which USA studies each of President Putin's moves. Pro-Assad, Anti-Assad, sympathisers of Turkey shooting down ally jets, empathiser of Russia retaliation. It does not matter which side Europe chooses; it matters that it chooses not to take a side. They can leave this to the UN. Switzerland has taught us neutrality works. Their only war is on the motorist, and this avoidance of conflict works well for them.

Europe, a former 6 country collaboration has grown to encompass many of the Soviet Union's former states which has been good for them. An interesting illustration as to why these countries want to be European is before me as I write this chapter in a local themed Diner situated in one of the older and more grandiose parts of Luxembourg City. On the wall hangs memorabilia such as advertising signs for household brand names. Among them is a picture of a lady bent over cleaning a red American car, possibly a Cadillac, but then, that's the only American mark that I really know (USA, please forgive my ignorance - as a Brit I have never really understood the American car market...). In the background is a sign "watch your curves, eat more beef". I presume the sign is aimed at promoting good honest healthy eating as we once knew it, because we know Americans are unaware that roads should have curves - Route 66 is a testimony to that!

Where this analogy comes together is that the emphasis was to eat beef to be full bodied - how different that has been the 21st Century! But I come to apply this to European economies and think it fits quite well: Being part of the European movement meant being full; a better option than being skinny and empty. Britain was once big and full (remember the Fifties).

Europe since its politico-economic creation, like a gluttonous carnivorous cow has eaten many of its skinny neighbouring counterparts, which actually has been good for those cows as some of them never learnt that it was bad to keep chewing on the electric barbed wire fence of low taxes and high Public salaries. Europe has been a sub-conscious bailout organisation to many countries without really knowing it. Essentially, Europe has been a venture fund; it invests in small nations hoping for above average growth by helping and teaching them how to run an economy. This has been a successful strategy.

The former eastern bloc countries chose Europe for many reasons, but the ability to export, grow and gain economic weight was definitely a major factor. Europe in recent generations has been stable enough to absorb these underweight economies, but Britain joined before Europe was really on its feet and while Britain itself was strong, lean and not wanting. The politicians during the late fifties and early sixties had the desire to keep the pace of growth high, but swayed between potential continued growth and the need to join. The 2016 referendum is now about Britain wanting, but   is   this   desire   one   that   will   bite   back?

3 UNIONS UNITED: UK IN THE EU

"Success is not final; failure is not fatal: it is the courage to continue that counts" –
Churchill

Europe saw the end of the war and the ensuing Marshall Plan backing the economies damaged to grow from the devastation left. Britain, under the political rule of Labour in 1951 looked to nationalise the coal, steel and heavy industries. The same time, the central European countries came together for a plan to essentially supra-nationalise these resources and the associated industries. There was of course then no real reason for Britain to give over the control of these resources in any way, shape or form to a supranational organisation. This was the basis for Britain's rejection of the initial European set up. Six years later saw the signing of The Treaty of Rome by the ECSC members with the aim of unifying the political and social set up of the partaking countries.

Britain was not looking to be politically influenced, legally governed, or socially run from elsewhere. Nor was it looking to lose its identity to just be 'European'. It wanted simply to continue growing, which meant trading internationally. Europe meant opportunities, but out of Europe meant exclusion. Britain tried to help Europe see that Free trade was sensible when done correctly and that it could be done on a global scale, and the creation of Europe was perfect timing for Britain, however the steps Europe took, albeit baby steps, were in the wrong direction.

For those of us old enough, or blessed with Fathers who introduced us to the awesomeness of British comedy of the Seventies and Eighties (Morecombe and Wise, the Two Ronnies, Open All Hours, Are You Being Served, Steptoe and Son, Porridge, Fawlty Towers etc.) we will remember the war-based sitcom Dad's Army and its map in which Britain aimed to

8

make progress across Europe to save it from the dreaded force. Britain, represented by the Union Flag in the shape of an arrow was of course not allowed to progress onto continental Europe but rather held back at its own shores. There are some striking parallels to be drawn as we look at Britain's participation in Europe.

The early sixties saw the arrival of the Beatles, however in spite of a hard day's work, British economy was on slow down. The relations with the commonwealth and the US were also slowing down, while the ECSC was gathering pace. Just like a sports car stuck behind a lorry on a motorway, Britain wanted to pull out and use the fast lane.

Britain tried to join the EU earlier than their actual inclusion, which took place in 1973. They tried twice, in fact. Once under Conservative power in 1963, and then again in 1967 under Labour. Ironically both times the moves were vetoed by Charles de Gaulle, a military and political man who sported rather a familiar moustache.

Prime Minister Harold Wilson held a one-day conference for the Labour party, which was then followed by a referendum in 1975 in relation to essentially the very same question Britain now faces: Should she stay in the EU? Labour voted at almost 2-1 to leave, however the referendum saw 67 per cent of the voters wanting to remain within the Europe, the EEC as it was then called.

Britain has since teetered on the brink of the EU since then and has only narrowly escaped (or missed out, in case you would like author impartiality) getting more involved as the EMU from the early nineties turned to the single monetary currency 'Euro' which was released in 2002. It made cents (cheap pun, I know) that the EMU would come to this point. Conservative want to be European, Labour leaders said that they are behind the idea of the currency, but would only move to include Britain once the time is right. No political party with any 'serious' (if ever that word could be used for a party of politicians) credentials has come forward in Britain.

The treaty of Lisbon which was signed in 2007 with the aim of altering the structures of the EU institutions so that the EU and its core values are better served. It was a reform subtly touching the very points Britain has for a long time stood against; that the labour laws change to become more European, which translates to working less thoughtfully; slower, and being better compensated. The country also has diminishing control over immigration and ultimately shows us the key point of Europe - which if Bryan Adams were to sing about it, he would sing "Everything he do, he do it for EU" - whatever Europe decides together aims to realise the dream of Schuman. It could have been taken as a hint for Britain to think about leaving.

An interesting comparison of growth and debt reveals that Britain has grown more than the EU since 2010, all the while British debt has quintupled. In spite of this, she still remains one of the stronger economies and therefore deserves to have the benefits that come with it. Britain wanting means that they overlook that she already has good benefits from being in the EU and the risk of voting to leave in the hope for better rights is a riskier one than a voter should look to take.

But if this Island did not rock the boat a little every now and then, The Declaration of Independence could not call the British 'The disturbers of our harmony'. The Islanders may disturb the peace once more in choosing where Britain wants to stand.

4 EUROPE: ONE SMALL STEP FOR THE COUNCIL...

The world doesn't change before your eyes; it changes behind your back. – Terry Hayes, I am Pilgrim

A few months ago I was driving a Maserati round the south of Italy while there for work. I had to travel at speeds unbeknown to Maserati because of the state of the roads. Yet just a few weeks earlier I was travelling through Germany unhindered by road quality (if I ignore the habitual, horrendous amounts of work on the Autobahn).

It is hard to imagine that at the same moment in time, both countries fought together in the same war, on the same side and that from the two of them it was Germany which took the biggest beating, yet has emerged the greater. What really caused this difference was that while both countries were willing to roll up their sleeves and aim to rebuild and work for its future, Germany was helped by its geographic location and governmental policies. Italy in recent years suffered under Berlusconi's antics, while Schröder's plan for Germany blossomed under Merkel's care and attention to look after not only itself, but the interests of Europe.

How this Germany is different to the one which stood by and helped Britain to crumble almost twenty five years ago. I hope the stresses they have suffered carrying Europe for over 50 years will not lead to another rejection of mercy, and the grouping of countries against the Great British cause.

The official European Union website *www.europa.eu* references one of the advantages of European integration is that in times of recession, EU countries can continue trading with one another and thus avoid the usual defensive pattern of focusing on domestic production. If being part of Europe really presents anti-recession opportunity, then it would be able to

11

stop any domestic recession. Two of the last things that a country needs during stagnation are a lack of control over the cost of their goods and a continued obligation to import. A lack of recycling its own wealth is one of the reasons for which a recession can occur. Another is the lack of being able to export because of quality and competitiveness.

The struggling country would need to either improve quality of their goods and services or failing that, reduce the cost of such goods. The ECB, who are the ones with the task of ensuring this claim, cannot do anything about the quality of the goods, and would not welcome the weakening of the currency, for just one country to avoid a continued domestic recession. This then leaves only active policies such as bond buying programs to stimulate growth in the faltering country.

A country's goods having quality issues compared to European counterparts will never be overturned unless an equal benefit can be found and this of course usually comes in the form of cheaper goods, partly caused by the country's weakened currency. Competitive neighbours would therefore rule out any help to such a country in times of recession. The promise, while well-meaning is based upon the fact that each partaking country would receive a certain amount of trade income through minimum exports, but that is a small consolation in a European slowdown.

As an economy with its own currency, Britain can essentially handle this risk through its own policy. The floating ability of the British currency is a very valuable jewel that must under no circumstance be relented. After all, it is Sterling. Removing this currency removes freedom of evolution within the country as different market sectors strengthen and weaken.

This loss of control of its own monetary policy has been at the forefront of the British mind during the past twenty five years, knowing that opting for the EMU, which is now the single monetary union would limit not only Britain's own voice by giving away sovereignty, but also growth through the limitation of goods trading. Lest we forget Black Wednesday, when Europe chose not to help even though Britain was part of both the EU and the ERM when it needed financial support.

However, for those countries whose Central Banks deal in terms of Euro, it does not appear to be all that it promises. Recession for the whole European area on the other hand, is hardly a worrying factor as approximately a quarter of the World GDP is from within the European Union, meaning that if Europe hits a recession it is likely that the rest of the world would be in the same general pattern.

Technically we see that if one group of weaker economies goes down then 'the richer countries' must pick them back up, and no one likes losing their tax money to causes which don't appear to have direct benefits to them. The mass expansion of the European Union in 2004 really did not help the UK opinion as it seemed like just increasing the size of a time bomb, with the inclusion of eastern European countries.

The danger is simple and ever present: Without the separation by currency, Britain would become separated only by island status - Geographically handicapped with only one hope of providing competitive trade prices: genetically modified monster-sized flying pigs which deliver and collect goods from the mainland for free. Or alternatively, provide better quality goods at a cheaper price - Easy.

The growing geographical and political period of the mid to late 20th century benefited Europe, with the opening of its doors to the movement of skilled workers. However even in these times of general growth and inflation within Europe, it is interesting to see that since the early 1980's, European growth has steadied and even reversed compared to that of America.

Factoring in inflation the actual annual growth rate has America leaving the Eurozone behind by a couple of percentage points for almost every one of the years. This low growth plus the issues European countries have had since the financial crisis have seen the easing of monetary policy to manufacture 'gentle inflation and growth'. This shows the true story: Europe manufactures more figures than it does progress.

In such a tight, low growth environment, large migratory influxes are suddenly not so welcome. Europe is not at its best and with no real confidence of a pickup in the economy. Give the current migrants the negative label "asylum seekers" and countries once aligned for the same goal shut their borders quicker than the lid of a cookie jar on the fingers of a thieving obese infant.

In separating people depending upon their birthplace or ancestry and current need, we actually close the doors to potential growth. I have watched the Asian community in England grow massively, not only through new arrivals, but reproduction; Britain post healthy economic figures in spite of an aging workforce. Without the migrants, many areas of the economy would have suffered.

These last years, I have watched Luxembourg continue to accept a growing Portuguese community which is now actually the majority here not just because of reproduction, but also random young people trying their chances here due to a lack of jobs in their home country. We can look and say bravo that these young entrepreneurs look to make something, and therefore should be embraced. Or alternatively, we could as united economies be there to encourage these young entrepreneurs to do business in their home country. After all, as Europe becomes generally over-populated, certain areas struggling for employment and growth are actually becoming under-populated.

In this instance, could Luxembourg not afford to, as part of Europe pay into a fund aimed at promoting young entrepreneurs to develop businesses within their home countries? Europe has the schemes out there to help entrepreneurs, but are they readily accessible to good business plans? I must say I am ignorant to the answer as I would need to find how each government present these opportunities. I know I risk sounding like the celebrity-status Presidential campaigner Donald Trump with a sort of "just build a wall all along the borders" attitude, but this couldn't be farther from the truth. I am not for seeing 'foreigners' leave, but rather that they be encouraged to support their local communities. While people do not spend money on goods when they have no income, they have no income because there are no jobs. This stimulus does not exist, and is in certain countries actually cramped by European policy. Europe is not to blame, but lax governance pre Euro. To share some background information on yours truly, I have benefited from open doors within Europe, and have thus been given the chance to give something back through many government and European schemes. I cannot say I have lacked for a thing during these periods and for that am most grateful.

Europe and its open doors means that certain countries are essentially an 'eat all you can' offer at your local pub, while other countries are in the alleyways going through the bins. As an EU citizen, one should be wary because the European economy doesn't really have a positive mid-term outlook. There is however positive data which I think is important to focus on; the best EU growth countries of the last decade have seen more people employed, but as of yet their productivities have declined. This is extra tax revenue and less expenditure for the government which can help to improve the infrastructure, and contains the potential research investment and then automation and increased efficiency leading to a positive efficiency.

EU has also increased its assets in relation to its GDP, but in reality it has only doubled its holding in the same period that America has tripled theirs. These assets are not a negative reflection of the Central Bank's need to bankroll the country, but rather a sign of stored wealth. The increase of Europe's holdings is however remaining steady when compared to GDP, and this is easier to achieve when there is a fairly stable growth and inflation rate; advantages of being large with active policies does mean peaks and troughs smoothed out stands for good reading on a graph.

This is good reading through rose-tinted glasses, but is actually just part of the problem which occurs with statistics thanks to loose monetary policy, a flag which Mario Draghi has been an advocate of waving in recent times as an attempt to stimulate growth. All this has done is delay the inevitable - like papering over the cracks - and prove the ECB does not really believe the EU can well handle a recession. A question is how much longer does Europe want to fight off the problem by manipulating statistics? I just hope they stop before they no longer can make use of the statistics in forecasts otherwise they won't see the next crisis coming. Maybe those ripples on the EU flag are just the cracks reappearing from behind.

Maybe the ECB are now just making up for lost time and by proving they are swift to react, as during the last crisis it took them too long to react the collapsing, while the Fed was straight on it by reducing interest rates. This allowed the US Policy Makers to work with the ensuing weakening and thus control the situation, the US have indeed come out all the better for it.

It seems the ECB suffers from a complex of some sort, almost like they are insecure to not be the best all-rounder, and in the long term it hurts the economy of the countries obliged to help. Europe has too many different styles managed by one set of policies. This essentially cramps certain countries and their way of domestic growth. The struggle the country then faces translates to the emigration of their younger workers. In a few generations, there will be a good blend of mixed cultures alongside each other, reducing the negativity of the stifling policies. But for now; Sovereign Britain equals Bespoke policies.

European data and hope is based on Germany continuing to carry the continent through, while the more rapidly growing economies, that is, those of the former Eastern bloc eventually increase their GDP to levels which can give a new drive to Europe. This would mean that ECB policy can get back to just being just supervisory, with occasional mild tweaks. It is excepted to take between three and six years for the Eastern bloc to move from producing less than 6 per cent of Europe's GDP to eventually producing 9 per cent - demographics recommend it should be 20 per cent for Europe to be truly developed. In the same time frame, Germany is likely to have the same GDP as France and Italy together. Remove Britain from the forecast calculations for the end of 2018 leaves the second and third largest EU countries providing only enough GDP to match that of the largest. This is a problem for Europe as the economy, aiming for almost 2 per cent inflation, rests firmly on very few governments. The continued weakness of the Mediterranean countries, plus weak French and Italian data do not stand for any improvement in these forecasts. Europe is essentially still emerging; but because of its size will struggle with its growth.

Germany, at the blink of an eye, appear to have been that constant European country; from starting up, getting things done, and keeping moving. I would expect that younger generations of European see it this way, and seems to be reflected in the fact that the last ten years has seen Germany gain on average 1 per cent GDP per capita against America, although what shocked me when checking statistics was that between the late 1980's and the global impact of the Housing crisis in 2007, Germany had been one of the worst performing European countries by GDP per capita, helped mainly by its lack of competitiveness.

Essentially, time spent being 'too good' in the early European years plus the reunification of Germany lead to weakened growth and thus unemployment began to rise. This however was the precursor to the structural reforms Germany underwent to emerge as a top World Economy of the 21st Century.

To ensure this is not a Europe bashing chapter, following are some points for a balanced perspective, proving Europe is not an also ran; the International Monetary Fund (IMF) put the GDP PPP (purchasing power parity) of Europe to a level just behind China, the world leader. Data does however show that since 2006 America has left Europe behind in terms of growth, despite their own results being weak; this progress is thanks to its effort to work with the situation, rather than fight it to stimulate a pre-defined target such as 'close to 2 per cent inflation'. Europe can easily achieve this if it works with. Like a good martial arts fighter who uses the opposition's strength to his own good; Europe can take the migrant crisis, the high debt levels and the Brexit issue to reform itself into a strong growing economy again. Given the size of Europe, both geographically and as a share of wealth, I am stumped as to how growth can come unless they remove the stifling regulations. Open doors to people does not always mean open minds to their ideas.

When we look at the geographic scale of America, Russia or China, Europe still does more than holds its own. America is a fully developed country, while Russia and China are still not truly developed. Europe can be the developed area that grows strongly, or a developing area which either grows strongly or drops off. Whichever side we look at Europe from, it is clearly helped and hindered because of the diverse cultures which create different interests within itself. If a Brit needs confirmation of the oxymoron these factors bring, he only needs to look at London.

Europe has enough of everything as long as the countries comprising the Union work together to handle the needs of those on its soil. In relation to the influx of people, aside from the efforts of Germany and a small handful of others whom have done more than their fair share to help sort the problems, we have sadly seen already the borders of several European countries shut to protect themselves. Can we as a Union help these countries whom only want to receive good? Europe, to certain countries is a charity in times of their need.

Some countries are in a bad state and are just holding on to the EU lifeboat, and a point to note is that if a country is in such a bad state that it can only look for help for itself, this is already better than countries which will *only* look for helping itself; this is then actually the first small step in helping others. At the Morgan Stanley Investment Management office in Luxembourg, I had the chance to see the computer screen of a gentleman carrying the sticker "the strong don't put down the weak, but rather help the weak to become strong". This of course was not his quote, but it summarises what should be the mentality of everyone.

The said gentleman in fact, is a product of mixed cultures himself and was the main highlight of my time there. A Serbian German working in Luxembourg. That sticker shows why Europe can be a superpower. And ultimately, how the acceptance of migrants can make Britain Great. The more immigrants Europe takes, the more it needs Europe to share the burden.

I remember one of the many stupid things I did during childhood was a 'scientific experiment' during bath time involving cold tap water and a hot lightbulb – and yes, it is exactly what you are thinking: I flicked copious amounts of cold water at the bulb until it eventually imploded. Impressive it was! The bulb parts came together with such force that it all shattered into a dangerous mess.

One could say then that like the light bulb - the European Union - is never far away from being a community-driven divided experiment; one which will eventually not be able to stand and thus will explode in spectacular fashion. Every political clash can escalate into the conflict needed to separate the union; like a nuclear power plant under the sleepy reckless finger of Homer Simpson…would anyone want to be near this Springfield we call Europe?

Britain though can only hope that in the event of an exploding Europe the waves will be big enough to push the island further away, like flotsam, but it will not be so easy if she is anchored to the mainland, because those on the shoes of continental will hold those guide ropes very tight.

One thing we can think about is that in most cases, the larger the experiment, the larger the fallout. I remember a chemistry lesson in which our wacky teacher wanted to demonstrate that group 'one' metals have larger reactions in relation to the increased number of electrons its atoms have. We never did convince him to throw a lump of Caesium into a bowl of water, but he did eventually throw Potassium into a glass bowl of weak Hydrochloric acid instead of just plain old boring water. I am not sure what he expected, but we enjoyed it as the vessel broke under the shock and the gushing water soaked his shoes. In spite of the unexpected result, the shock, the deluge and ensuing mess, the worst that the teacher received was wet feet. Something that could actually be laughed off. I hope that the metaphorical British diving flippers are readily stored somewhere safe for when this vessel Europe relents.

5 REFERENDUM: KNOWING THE REFERENCE

"To know the answer, a wise man first understands the question" – Monnie Quatsch

The need to renegotiate has been stoked by the immigration crisis from Syria. Europe is taking the brunt of the migration and will not be able to get them on the boats and across to America before Donald Trump's protective wall is finished. Each country worries how it can house such a large influx of people in a short space of time.

I remember Richard Littlejohn wrote a book called 'To hell in a handcart'. It touched on the erm, joys of being in Europe with an open door policy. If Britain chooses to wait until Europe fails, a handcart isn't much good on the highway to hell. And that is where a crashing Europe will go.

The initial question for the referendum: "Should the United Kingdom remain a member of the European Union" has been amended to: "Should the United Kingdom remain a member of the European Union or leave the European Union?" for the sake of impartiality. This is something Britain loves to do. Busybodies finding reasons to pick fault in terms, and find slants in the way people present things. Europe, does not yet suffer this problem. Europeans are ignorant of mind tricks, or at least ignorant of how to play them.

Regularly over the last ten years, people holding different passports ask me why Britain "doesn't not want to join Europe?" (to convey their tone of question feel free to read as 'refuses to join Europe', 'hates Europe' and 'wants to be different'). I am but one man, with little influence and a handful of possibly incorrect opinions. Ignoring the fact that Britain is already in Europe, I have learnt the best response is "Europe? Why does it want us?" I guess therefore we can see ourselves as different, after all,

Europeans see us that way.

The Pound of course sets Britain apart and is most likely what these people from the Eurozone mean. After all, southern European economies were saved by taking the Euro. Well, actually the problems were just delayed, but long enough that ignorance could lead to the two events not crossing their minds. The fact of the matter is that Britain is a group of islands. These islands are all essentially on the outer section of Europe, and on the other side from the most rapidly growing part of Europe. These are obvious logistical disadvantages. The only change for Britain being in Europe for the transport is that lorries are no longer blocked at the port by the French. Hang on, that has happened several times since Britain has been part of Europe... (I write this as the French airport workers are on strike, and also there is no petrol to be bought in France, anywhere)

There are several exceptions found in Europe due to geographical location. Many countries are on the periphery, and none of them contain the either of the two people driving the European interest as much as France's Francois Holland and Germany's Angela Merkel. Denmark and Bulgaria are just some of the exceptions when it comes to the currency. They are both in the EU, yet retain their own currency.

In avoiding the single currency, Bulgaria can avoid the slowdowns from Europe while benefiting from Europe. This is essentially Europe circa 1951, and where Europe should have drawn its line. Ironically, when the world crashed and recovered; Bulgaria GDP of the 21st Century increased by more than 300 per cent; that is four times more than they produced in 2000. But before attributing this to the EU inclusion, that only happened in 2007, after they had already almost tripled their growth. Their membership in NATO showed the world they were a former communist country trying to break their ties with undertones. Just recently, Bulgaria reiterated that there is no interest for them to join the single currency; an echo of their 2012 statement. This poor country, the poorest in Europe sees the struggles they will face in trying to join the Euro. Sweden, another exception to the Euro rule has a GDP four times that of Luxembourg, which itself is the second richest country in the world in terms of GDP per capita. Essentially luxembourg wealth works for its people, Sweden have had an interesting monetary policy which has helped their country struggle a little.

Maybe Britain is different because English is such a widely spoken language, that everything else just seems foreign? This could affect the mentality of the Brit towards Europe. It could also be the reason Europeans think British do not want to be European. I have no idea if this is the case for some, but I know enough English people that will not venture farther east than Ipswich for a holiday. As for me, I was raised with a French teacher as a mother thus every year was a France road trip. I have come to like learning languages, and I am currently using children's fairy tales narrated in Hindi to learn the language.

Maybe it is just the mentality of a Brit and a European. Europe puts an emphasis on end result information; know the answer in case you are asked. Britain puts an emphasis on understanding the problem at hand, so that the answer can be worked out. It is what the British call common sense and logic. People may find this strange, but I can assure you I have seen this far too much for it to be irony.

I was found a few months ago browsing the Official Journal of the European Commission. I thought it would have been a good read to help me sleep, but actually I found that my mind couldn't switch off because the time had been taken to define so many things. Sure, there are business rules needed to be put in place in every project, but the details of certain sizes of Diggers and Tyres that are acceptable for Plant Machinery? I thought these would be best defined by the companies themselves who choose to build these things? After all, that is competition, and how technology advances. I came away thinking that the European Commission was there only to stop competition and to favour those countries located in the Central Europe, the founders of the idea. After all, they are closest to all for transport costs.

But surely this cannot be a huge experiment to move more power to the already most powerful. Really, could they be audacious enough to try and pull the wool over so many eyes in one go? Maybe being that island a bit farther away gave us a better view.

So to be an exception can have its hindrances, but I do not see it as negative. Just as when a friend refers to you as 'different'? It is really a compliment, and seems a much better antonym to 'you bore me', after all, they are your friend. However, I do only enjoy hearing it when I know the person is being genuine. Last week I sat down with a member of the Luxembourgish Public Office. We had never met before, and I was asked some personal questions about my life; why I live in Luxembourg, what I do, what is the next step for my life etc. I revealed a little of my past, of dreams shattered and the picking up of all the pieces which were left. Two hours later, and the gentleman remarked it was an interesting and refreshing time talking with me.

To bring the comparison together; am I different? Maybe, but does it change how I should be treated? Maybe. After all, there are many world views, many cultures and many opinions. This open-mindedness is needed with each person one comes into contact with, and in reality, countries are much like people; the cultures are their characters. A country based on greed and corruption cannot be trusted to pay off emergency loans. A country intent on partying and desperate to look good to others cannot be left alone with monetary policy.

Where does Britain's referendum fall into this? Several countries within the EU do not see the need to go farther with Europe other than open trade. Seven of the twenty eight members do not have the Euro. Several 'geographically European' countries do not take part in the EU: Switzerland and Norway to name a couple of household names.

These aren't exactly what we call developing nations! Norway boasts the largest sovereign wealth fund in the world, and Switzerland, albeit through some special attitudes to financial regulations holds plenty of money which in turn allows tax on profits. Tax which is lower than most around the world because of their special regime which taxes wealthy non-residents based on the expenditure rather than their earnings. A complex system designed to benefit certain people, allowing for a drawdown in the amount of tax levied on general goods.

Britain, reluctantly took part in the common market by accepting decimalisation (now that wasn't so hard was it? It was definitely easier for me as a child to accept to count in tens, rather ha'pennies, shillings and farthings – although I do still translate my weights into stones, pounds and ounces...). Now she will be called to fully embrace the rest. If she accepts, it will be easier said than done because no one wants to spend their working day measuring tomatoes to see if they are round, or can actually be sold for much more as 'flat tomatoes'...but then at least it is a job, which can be done badly and slowly for a better salary than it should be and a minimal risk of losing the job, thanks to Europe's laws.

For those unaware of why I mention this, what I have noted having worked in Luxembourg - a hub of Europe and a cross road of cultures which gives an insight into the best and worst of the different cultures - many people fear losing their job so they simply do not make the effort they should for their employer to avoid risking their position. The best way to avoid losing your job is to have a consistently low work rate. It sounds stupid, but if the monitoring of team members is based only on who makes the mistakes, one can work slowly and avoid being on the list. I am however pretty certain that no successful business person got to where they are with a strategy like that! Britain unlike Europe, offers the chance to lose your job, and a weak unemployment aid to follow. This is a great incentive to work harder and this a character trait I hope she never gives up. But in some situations, it is true that much fuss does not equal extra efficiency, as Ernest Hemmingway would tell us:

"Never confuse movement with action"

Such a book should deliver an insight into what Britain needs to 'fix'. To evaluate what needs to be fixed, Britain needs to know what it is doing to invest in the future. Honestly, I think what needs to actually be asked is not whether Britain stays or goes, but simply does Britain want to go where Europe is heading?

Everybody knows a developing market struggles to develop without a decent infrastructure. It is why Myanmar has such huge roads in an almost empty capital. It is why China has a high speed train nowhere. It is conversely why Brazil refuses to emerge, but rather wastes each year in the hope that the price of their main resource, iron, matches that of Gold.

The British infrastructure is close to failing and can easily fail if the government is not careful. Public Transport is expensive, and the city roads are crowded; the amount of time spent blocked on roads adds a cost on items which could otherwise be avoided.

A year of these costs could easily be rerouted to avoid later issues, after all a stitch in time saves nine. Not that this chief procrastinator can say much about that. I spent months ignoring toothache until the tooth cracked. Four dentist visits and 2,300 Euros of bills later, I found my new tooth is not ideal. If I had sorted the tooth when I first got the pain it would have been an easy filling. If I had known the discomfort awaiting me I would have done something about it, and not just flowed with the course of time. Britain, can fix its tooth now.

In Hamlet, Laertes tells to Ophelia that:

"Best safety lies in fear"

This depth of study into Europe and its position both domestically and within the EU is needed so that the risks will be seen, weighed, and then acted upon. Now it is motivation time. To set about the plan for the future encompassing education, health service, infrastructure and government spending, whichever party be in power needs to stand by it instead of the country flip flopping inefficiently between the policies. Once the nation chooses whether to stay or go, it is the duty of its citizens to back the government in achieving this reform.

Britain sent a lot across to America in its 'birth', so now we can have something back from them; the Ralph Waldo Emerson quote:

"In skating over thin ice, our safety is in our speed."

Since Europe's steady drop from 2012 to now staring into the abyss, we have seen a massive diversion in trade balance between the UK partners, split into EU and non EU. We are running a large trade deficit with EU countries, whereas a healthy positive balance with non-EU countries.

Getting out of Europe now is like deciding not to climb on the Titanic, because you suddenly fear you might get sea sick. Britain is thinking about leaving to stop migration, but that is entirely the wrong reason to leave altogether. Britain can get out now with very little damage, or can remain a part of it and wait for that iceberg called EU debt to smash into smithereens.

If Britain decides to be that hero who comes to Europe's rescue again, then it can. But it must first count the cost. Europe will not be as damaged as it could be, by us, or another, or even a couple of the larger economic powers leaving. After all, the depreciation which the Euro will receive in the event of a parting of ways will allow the European economy to recover its debt by means of selling off its foreign wealth. During this period, other economies would benefit on the cheaper goods, and these in turn would actually prop up the economy. Europe could be like a captain of a sinking ship who will not abandon it. But the worst that could happen is Europe is captained by nations who do not alert its voyagers so that they all on for so long that eventually everyone drowns.

One thing British voters need to pay attention to is to not think back to the Europe that was. Europe has evolved. Much has changed, like as is expected from such a large project. The job offering alone for all the bureaucracy has helped relocate much wealth to the pockets of well compensated European Commission workers. This is maybe a fairy tale ending to Schuman's dream.

Rapunzel would still be stuck in that tower if she had not taken the opportunity to get out when she had the chance. Could there really ever be a   better   opportunity   for   Britain   to   leave?

6 MIGRATION, IS THAT ALL WE FEAR?

"The only thing we have to fear is fear itself" – Franklin D. Roosevelt

Beginning his solemn inaugural speech of 1933 during America's great depression, FDR stated the above comment and immediately followed it with:

"Nameless, unreasoning, unjustified terror which paralyses needed efforts to convert retreat into advance..."

In the current climate of war in the Middle East and threats on the west through terror, the eyes with which Western Europe views the 'migration crisis' may at times be sceptical. It even gives another dimension to President Roosevelt's quote when its context is removed. It only takes a couple from the millions coming across from Syria to underpin the fears and stereotypes – just a couple of terrorists is enough to strike fear into the hearts of a nation - yet calculated as a percentage of terrorists compared to the number of incoming people, there is actually a higher percentage of murderers currently sat in Britain's jails. I would however not be surprised if a number of people in Britain think that getting out of Europe will distance itself from potential attacks. It will not, and neither will it help to stop these violent evil atrocities from happening in Europe.

If there were one single factor which can be said to have really triggered the desire to leave for the majority of the 'leave' voters, it would have to be this issue of immigration at a time of so much uncertainty. But in reality, if there is no uncertainty somewhere then there is no reason for a substantial migratory flow. Immigration is an easy term to throw about without it actually meaning anything, but at the same time the way in which it is thrown about really does show a person's bias. One of the last effective reasons for Britain leaving is to try and decrease the levels of immigrants. I know it is what really sparked the referendum, but it will not be fixed by it. To underpin my belief that British people are fed up with the perceived continual influx, I fully expect that the upcoming football tournament between 'European' countries will see a lot of violence from those wearing the St George on a shirt. To add tension to any potential conflict, this tournament is in France... I believe this will be just enough to not only stain the nation and thus the whole of Britain's reputation, but also will open European eyes to if they really want Britain in Europe.

As for the benefit of a migrant to a country, this should be calculated in relation to the person's economical value. Their acceptance into the country should however include the social factors of the person's need. For example, an ideal holiday maker is ultra-short term direct growth to the economy in which he vacations and is accepted into a country as such. He arrives, he spends, and he leaves (Hooligans excluded, of course). To mention holiday makers under migration may seem strange, but it is done to emphasise that they usually bring only benefits, because the negatives of cost and burden are already taken care of in the preparation of the area as a tourist location.

Migrancy is a different issue because the general benefit from the presence is only felt later, and therefore the understanding of the situation is important. Emigrants from the UK can be families whose Father or Mother receives a job abroad meaning that the family relocates. If we consider a family such as this, the continued business which the family gives is the benefit. A family in the financial position to do this is obviously a good thing for the economy where they go. It could be an elder couple looking to set up a holiday home as a permanent base. If we consider such a couple who go without need to work, then the benefit is limited. There would be no employer to profit on their labour and no income tax paid on their salaries.

Immigrants of a young age on the other hand, present the opportunity of not only working, but spending. Once he works, he earns and he can spend. The low skilled immigrant is actually a good thing - as long as the influx is not excessive - as this helps to keep low the prices of basic goods. Even with minimum wage laws, factories and the like can benefit from their desire to work in any way possible to earn a living. This keeps both cost of living and inflation from rising too quickly. This benefit Britain is now overlooking, even though it has a lower cost of living than most EU countries in relation to its GDP. The high skilled worker on the other hand, brings the obvious advantage of increasing the quality of what is being offered. Both of these types of migrants are needed, unless of course the population is growing rapidly enough from domestic reproduction – something Britain is not doing.

When looking at statistics on the reproduction figures throughout

Europe, Latin countries are providing more than one child per household than a British family. In addition, the Latin family starts at an earlier age. Neither of these facts will knock you off your feet, but this is nonetheless a double effect to overpopulation within their own countries, yet the emigration of many young adults from the likes of Spain and Portugal to other European countries ensures the country of origin does not suffer the effects as much; essentially the rest of Europe absorbs the impact of their decisions.

Without the growth of the population, new businesses would have a hard time hiring as the unemployment rate would be low and the average working age would keep increasing. This would in turn be an upward pressure on salaries and eventually the consumer end prices. China started to suffer this is the last decade and as a result, despite better efficiency in manufacturing goods, the cost of labour actually drew down the profit margins and eventually forced higher prices; higher prices which meant other developing Asian nations could provide competition. This was the basis for the Chinese economic slowdown which eventually came to a head as an overleveraged foreign investor stock market deleveraged and then panicked. There are two Stock markets in China and the ensuing crash brought more realistic prices of the international investor market, as it aligned with the domestically offered stock market. The population and slowdown were both well presented already back in 2012 by Ruchir Sharma in his book 'Breakout Nations'.

One part of the British worry about large net migration inflows is housing, especially when Britain is "overcrowded". This is something heard regularly, and does have some validity. "The houses are fairly small compared to those in Europe", is something else I have heard, and while it is true that I have seen areas in Britain with small houses, it is also true that I have witnessed areas with generally larger houses than in Europe. One thing I have noticed however is the lack of apartments in most of the mid-size British towns I have visited.

Britain can claim it does not have place for more people. But then the majority of towns do not have the persons per square foot as other large European towns. A memory I have from all my childhood holidays to France is the fact so much of the country was rural. It is 248k m^2 and houses 66 million. The UK is 243K m^2 and houses 64 million people. There is not much difference in these figures, which actually surprised yours truly as I expected France to be quite a bit larger in terms of surface area, even than all the UK.

It does show there is room to physically accommodate more citizens. Could Britain then look to provide for some of Europe's inflows? We naturally do not want to destroy areas of such beauty as the Snowdonia mountains, the Lake District, the Pennines, the Yorkshire Moors, the

Grampians, the Cairngorms etc. but certain mid-size towns could be built a little more vertically. There remain enough brown-field sites, especially in the north of England; the area worst hit during Britain's tango with Europe and its ERM. These sites can be converted into offices and apartments so that in the event that Britain stays in Europe, incentives can be offered for international companies to move there. If the break from Europe is chosen, then the government can still find schemes to fill these areas with subsidised businesses. The housing issue is something that will need to be addressed sooner or later anyway, regardless of the referendum result.

As an Englishman I am aware one's home is his castle, and as a child I had believed that when I grew up I would have a crocodile infested moat which would keep all aspects of my childhood fantasy lifestyle safe.

Having therefore to share accommodation for my first couple of years in Luxembourg, and even latterly having my own apartment, living with neighbours has meant that I have had to humble myself and accept I cannot have a detached house with garden both front and back, nor a trampoline next to my heated swimming pool hedged in by conifer trees. I was raised in a 1970's semi-detached house of a leafy suburb with an attitude to respect my neighbours, especially in regards to the volume a stereo could be played at. The hardest part of learning to live in a building with other residents is knowing that above, below and to the sides there are residents who can hear everything you do much more readily that if one lived in a detached house. But this is also the price I pay for having a view over the whole of Luxembourg's city centre. My stereo is still played louder than I need, without interfering with my neighbour's daily lives.

To prepare for the migrant influxes, the government could allow those towns needing the most generation or where there are several factory type businesses be given certain residential buildings to be rented out as short term subsidised schemes. This is then a cost prepared in advance, which is cheaper than emergency reactions.

I am far from suggesting building projects such as Le Corbusier's 1952 Unité d'habitation: The Swiss Architect designed this striking building for Marseilles, and it is possibly the building most used as a representation of an impoverished life in Marseilles. This 'vertical city' is a long concrete rectangle in France with a very stark appearance – to understand just what I am referring to, google the building. I am also against Skyscrapers for towns; as dramatic as they can be – they should be reserved for certain locations such as financial or city centres. There is however always the possibility of creating three and four storey housing, which can house at least a handful of apartments. This is a great step in getting young couples onto the property ladder, before they become a two up two down family. The only negative in this case is the potential slowdown in the house prices, however, in terms of an investment house prices generally advance at a greater pace than the interest rates.

The population growth per annum of between 0.2 per cent and 0.6 per cent is a boost to the economy as it allows prices to remain competitive, while also the youthful age of the new citizens allows a reduction in the working age population and a chance to benefit from their longer years of working which they still have to complete. While 500 000 people enter Britain in a year, the net flow is actually just round 200 000. Comparing this to a population of 60 million we see it is only 0.3 per cent growth. Therefore, the issue is not about being able to place the potential workers, but the cost of housing them, preparing them for work, and supporting their family members which will not or cannot work. Once we remove those other factors such as fear and prejudice, we find ourselves at the real heart of the issue.

Essentially, leaving Europe may not deter the non-EU immigrant from coming; in fact, it may speed up the rate as people try to make it onto her shores before that door closes. It would however deter the EU migrants from coming. Interestingly, the net inflow which has occurred over the last ten years has seen an increase only of EU migrants.

The number of EU migrants to Britain per year is now around 250,000. Almost double that of 2004 and earlier. The total net immigration to Britain was around 50,000 a year during the 1990's. This drastic increase was brought about by the Labour Party's changing of the law in the late Nineties.

The world population growth, to put this inflow in perspective is a growth of 1.5 per cent per annum. Britain therefore is only gaining one fifth in relation to the global population. Britain essentially still has it quite well, but Europe does have many of its countries producing negative growth figures. Understandable, as young couples and single adults are leaving several countries in search of the good life in the richer European countries.

Britain aims to therefore slow the migration into its country, but does so under the very watchful eye of Brussels, who can and will jump at the slightest hint possible untoward treatment. In order to slow migration, stricter rules and essentially hindrances or 'punishments' on those trying to enter have been proposed. (While I try and not give bias throughout the book, I will here state that personally I am against refusing welfare to migrants. However, I do believe in their being controls on financial aids).

Such proposals have included no child benefits to immigrants for a certain time period, and a red card scheme which allows a blanket stop on immigrants if the burden is getting too great. There are no better ways being proposed to stop the inflow to Britain, unless other countries are more accommodating in terms of taking their 'fair share'. But how can a country such as Spain with 20 per cent unemployment take a fair share? If fair is calculation in terms of current population or rate of unemployment, then Britain will have a larger share than most to bear.

The only other option is to have an economy which weakens so much that it is one of the least interesting economies to migrate to. Something, Britain is obviously not willing to have and for good reason. Brexit, may slow slightly the migrant influx, but short term it will definitely slow any growth of GDP.

Just in case this idea gets picked up by the British Government and they need to brainstorm some ideas how to achieve this, then I suggest a bit of slanted statistics reports to be circulated letting the rest of the world know how bad the UK is, such as crime figures, country debt and any other statistics needed to help discourage the potential immigrant, especially an EU immigrant.

In the case of a Brexit, deterrents to EU migrants into Britain would be the extra legislation needing to be fulfilled by a potential EU migrant, and Britain leaving the EU will not only scare some away from being stuck in limbo, but will immediately weaken the economy enough to deter more potential migrants and then as such the problem is better handled, albeit on a secondary basis.

Staying in Europe with better controls - as Cameron is trying to convince people he is fighting for - may stop migrancy from growing so rapidly however it does not show promise, not even to hold at bay the yearly figures around 250,000 migrants each from EU and non EU countries. It most certainly does not show hope to achieve the 100,000 net inflow he claims to be aiming for.

If Europe's slowdown and thus weakening will force people to look to the stronger EU countries as a place of domiciliation, such as Britain, staying in Europe will only delay the problem some years.

And this global slowdown is already upon us. Coupled with the amount of debt leveraging a typical family from a Western European country has and which will need to be corrected will also be a pressure for European migration. Many of these migrants see Britain as a haven and an exception. This, as a note to European readers, is why Britain feels it can demand better deals from Europe.

To summarise, the migration levels slowed just a little would be a controlled positive boost to the working age population and therefore the future GDP of the UK, while the second generation migrants also allow for a diversification of business ideas. Currently, it is the extra costs around the worker's family which risk becoming a burden and essentially aid the British economy to stall.

British citizens must decide if the healthy competition for jobs is worth the weakening spending power of the average home. By remaining in Europe and keeping its borders open, Britain can also keep their hearts open to the needs of these families whom currently have been reduced to not   knowing   what   living   is.

7 SOVEREIGNTY, LEGISLATION AND THE RIGHT TO TRADE

"Legislation is the pre-cursor to absent mindedness" – anon

Reality is best regarded from every side, so for a Brit to better understand what Britain is called to implement or has avoided from taking part in, it might be interesting to recap the development of 'Europe', although probably not.

Aimed at avoiding war by the trading within a common market, Europe, as a political and economic institution was conceived. 6 countries from what was then the centre of the continent came together to share the Coal and Steel plan; one which would see the open free trading of certain resources.

This plan was not just a simple agreement to that end. It was actually a four layered plan, because the simple proposal was rejected. Apparently the easiest way to organise this was in fact the most complex way.

The four layers were designed to answer theoretically the following problematic, or that is, until it came into practice;

How to manage the community, how to interfere with the institutions within the participating countries, how to tamper with the economic and social provisions and then finally any meddling that could be done in general.

In 1957, Euratom was created with the same idea as the ECSC except for nuclear resources. In the same year the Treaty of Rome was signed between the countries coming into force in 1958; this was the EEC (which later changed its name to EC, and then the European Union – there was obviously some complexity here, but for simplicity's sake, lets ignore it).

Naturally all of these advancements led to the simple structuring of 1 high court, 2 commissions, and 3 councils. It was as simple as 1, 2, 3, – proof that chaos does have an order.

Seeing that this European community experiment seemed to be working, in 1965 it was thankfully simplified with the Treaty of Brussels; the commissions, councils and high court structures were replaced with 1 commission and 1 council. To help the financial oversight, there was also a single operative budget set up. Europe was taking shape, while Britain was slowing down.

The United Kingdom who at this point was only a Free Trade partner, rather than an EU member, suggested a transatlantic set up however this was rejected. I think this would have been just common sense that doors should be open to trade with other countries if it is for the best. After all, why have limitations if it is a positive move. But then logic would have me say that because I have grown up in an era which has had open trade. I knew and understood from a young age this concept of open borders; for example, I could buy my penny sweets from any shop I wanted. I was not limited to a certain chain, but rather only limited to good economic sense. If you get the most or the best for your money without losing too much time, then it is worthwhile. But naturally the UK's proposal needed Europe to agree on it, document it, make it more complex, then sign on it. It did not come to fruition.

Set up in 1960 and running parallel to the EEC, was the EFTA (European Free Trade Association). This allowed countries to have agreements with 'Europe' for trading. Austria, Denmark, Norway, Portugal, Sweden, Switzerland and the United Kingdom were the partakers. In 1966 the EFTA countries achieved a full free trade agreement of industrial products.

Over the next fifty years, some countries came to the EFTA and then went as they moved on to full membership within the EEC. To this date, no country has left the EFTA to have less of a role in the EU. Britain could be the first, although Switzerland did vote by referendum in 1992 to refrain from joining the EU.

Denmark and the UK left the EFTA at the end of 1972 to join the EU from 1973, while Ireland made the jump straight into the EU. The 1980's saw Greece, Spain and Portugal join the EU also – three countries with a penchant for populating, and midday naps.

Alongside the EFTA was the creation of the EEA (European Economic Area), which was initially aimed at the free trade of fish and fishing rights between the EFTA countries in 1989. Six years later the EU saw the arrival of the EFTA countries Austria, Finland and Sweden.

Now that half of geographical Europe was involved in Europe (Union, that is), it was becoming time to include the European countries that Europe forgot since World War Two. 2004 saw the arrival of ten more countries; Czech Republic, Estonia, Cyprus, Latvia, Lithuania, Hungary, Malta, Poland, Slovakia, Slovenia. The EEA was also enlarged, in keeping with the EU link.

2007 saw the arrival of Romania and Bulgaria into the EU. I remember the news of their joining was not taken well by my family and friends of the family. Romania was synonymous with poverty as for over a decade several charities tried to help rebuild a country broken by the former dictator Ceausescu.

I remember hearing from my elders that the inclusion of these countries marked the demise of Europe, and the immigration crisis of Britain. Both have not happened, and now I can (albeit on seldom occasions) practice my (very bad level of) Romanian without having to travel to one of my favourite European countries. Croatia have since joined the EU.

The Free Trade Area grew when among others; Chile, Jordan, Lebanon, Mexico, Singapore and Turkey, came to the party. Just forty years later, it seemed that the United Kingdom's suggestion was taking place.

The 1960 attempt to open international barriers for trade may not have been accepted by the then European Union, but it did allow for the creation of the EFTA, which in turn led the way for the FTAs in place today.

I have named the chapter Sovereignty, Legislation and the right to trade. This is a trident of identity factors offered to those who are free. I say this because Sovereignty is not only the ability of a state to do as it best chooses for its people, but is the right to express this through its legislation, so that its population can purchase what they can afford within the said legislation.

The right for British to be British is something lives have been lost for, and something many people are proud of. In the days when the currency was in the form of commodities, resources and skills, free trade abound. Since the acceptance of specific currencies as not only a legal form of tender, but the granted way of trading, the freedom of trade has declined. Even the creation of a strong pound à la Thatcher did not free Britain from these bounds. But at least she summarised it well, that:

"The sterling is the greatest expression of sovereignty"

Only by appreciating the European vision, can the British vow to stay be best understood.

Having studied the judicial set up of both the Islands and the continent, I noticed that the structures at the very base are quite different. This is one of the subtle things Britain would need to change if it accepts to stay in Europe without being granted further Opt outs. Then there is the Parliamentary system - eventually pressure to hand over the main decision taking will be relented to the EU due to its insistence that Britain accept

European laws in all areas.

This is a problem, not that Europe will bring many laws against the British moral code, but because many laws are extra rules to standardise certain things. The amount of extra regulation implemented in European countries which is otherwise not needed is crazy, but it justifies the costs in the EU budget. I live the effects of these regulations first hand, and I see that in Luxembourg people ignore the law far more than in Britain. It is almost like the extra law the public must live by, the more it weakens their respect to it. Another issue is, and I mean this not in a dishonourable way, but the central European school systems are not designed to teach common sense, but rather simple data memory.

Britain does not have the reputation in Europe for having a good education system; this is not because it is bad, but rather it takes common sense to see just how useful the system is. Several British universities can boast a great level of teaching found almost nowhere else in the world. Britain does not need these extra rules to be implemented – Britain can and will surely be keeping abreast of current affairs and if Europe creates a law which is useful, or that would affect the exportable products be produced such as heavy plant machinery; the relevant companies would be taking note – this is after all, good business practice.

Law is made up of many sectors, from Civil Law, through farming laws to privacy laws. 65 per cent of current UK law is actually made in Brussels. While this seems huge, one needs to remember that a large percentage are legislative laws rather than a moral code or heinous crime related laws.

If one then takes the UK domestic laws, only around 15 per cent are actually influenced by Brussels. Being in Europe means Britain is subject to many more rules. Leaving would obviously not make Britain a lawless country, but would actually mean no more mindless restrictions or guidelines. There was a lot of UK law pre-EU membership, yet the country worked.

Britain can benefit from splitting now, as she has the chance to take the best of these 'extra laws', and can therefore better handle new domestic laws as needed. Just like an emerging economy can learn from previous experience, the UK can profit from not only having seen or heard about these additional laws, but having actually taken them for a test ride. After all, the one who leads the way stumbles first.

At a EUROFI Conference in 2015, in which one of the subjects was the need for more regulation in the financial sector to avoid another crash, some of the debaters chose this as a good idea to ensure that the markets are controlled. Eventually a British man who looked a little impatient with the way the debate was going pointed out the most obvious issue: If a company uses common sense as to how they manage their finances and operations, then there is no need for extra regulation. All the regulation does is strangle efficient businesses, and drag out the deaths of the inefficient businesses. In the end, we will have so much regulation that there will be almost no difference between financial institutions.

In 1992, Britain avoided implementation of some laws and agreements by opting out of the Treaty of Maastricht that was for the EMU. 1997 saw the Treaty of Amsterdam also have an opt out clause for Britain. This is the Schengen convention which not only has brought great advantages of being able to move freely between countries, it has also brought the great disadvantages of the wrong people moving freely between countries; the organisers of the Paris and Brussels attacks of 2015 and 2016 for example.

Britain also originally opted out of the Treaty of Lisbon in 2007 regarding justice and home affairs, however then subsequently opted in for thirty five of the hundred and thirty measures. This was not the best way to make friends, and friends make for easier trade negotiations, and ultimately, for better trade. Britain, interestingly is one of the most faithful and punctual countries in implementing the new laws to which the EU subjects it.

Treaties and partaking in Europe is all well and good, but less than 50 per cent of British imports come from EU, and more telling, 58 per cent of trade through exports is to non-EU countries. These relationships have changed by approximately 9 per cent in the last decade, in spite of more countries becoming part of the European union. These would be yet stronger figures in regards to the non EU trading, however the continued strengthening of the EUR from its inception, right until 2009 meant that EU countries could continue to profit from the hedging of their British imports. Since 2012 when the Pound strengthened back by over 20 per cent, British trade has plummeted with Europe.

3-4 million British jobs depend on UK export. That is just more than 10 per cent of the working population of Britain. This is a scary figure at first sight, and one that will be used to ensure a vote to stay is secured. But if we reduce this to its basis; this figure is the total. The office for national Statistics quotes 31.4 million employed in the last three months to February 2016. Imagine 30 per cent of these export-reliant jobs are lost, which is not going to happen, we start to see it its now around 4 per cent increase in unemployment. The cost of an unemployed person to the government is much less than that of an unemployed person in other Western and Central European countries.

To put this in perspective, unemployment benefits in Luxembourg total at least 80 per cent of the former salary (averaged over the last three months). Germany is at approximately 60 per cent, France is up to 70 per cent. Britain is closer to 25 per cent. She can therefore handle unemployment better than other countries. And thus, it is still not going to reach anywhere near a drastic burden; even with the very unlikely 4 per cent increase.

The current set up for Britain in the EU is that it must pay both Tariffs and Quotas when trading within the EU. Like the mafia, there is an honorary payment whenever a deal goes down. And in typical government fashion, the more the value of the trading, the more expensive trading gets. I guess that's the reason the EU can have gold stars on its flag. As Morocco from The Merchant of Venice received a shock upon reading a scroll from Portia, so to could Britain receive a shock from Europe:

> *"All that glisters is not gold —often have you heard that told.*
> *Many a man his life hath sold*
> *But my outside to hold.*
> *Gilded tombs do worms enfold.*
> *Had you been as wise as bold,*
> *Young in limbs, in judgment old,*
> *Your answer had not been inscrolled.*
> *Fare you well. Your suit is cold —*
> *Cold, indeed, and labor lost."*

8 THE DEAL?

"Friends are those who help in times of need. What I have learnt is that in times of need, one realises his time was spent with enemies" – Monnie Quatsch

Writing this during the build up to the country's decision on the 23rd June 2016 whether to remain in Europe, the markets have been historic, the media attention unprecedented, smaller European economies vocal, larger economic countries silent (shivering with worry, is my guess) because so much appears to be at stake.

Could Cameron carry us through, or can this boldness he is trying to display backfire like his Greek counterpart Alexis Tsipras in 2015. Even, could the berated Corbyn be of help; not from the opposition bench, but as politicians united for the good of the kingdom?

Britain, the Great; a small island which has since mediaeval times, fought above its weight. Britain has been here before. Fight for peace, but end up in war. A true leader arose in the fight against the German onslaught on Poland. Not only looking after Europe, but with America gave it to the Italians and Japanese also. They don't like it up 'em, Corporal Jones of Dad's Army fame would enthuse about the great Churchill style, yet in spite of the cost, Britain remained great.

How nice it would be to start this chapter looking at what Britain can debate to receive, but in reality it is the rest of Europe whom discuss Britain's deal. At least there will be impartiality in the deal discussions, after all Britain is a good friend of Europe. Except for the people who do not understand why Britain does not want to 'join', and also those people who do not understand 'why Britain wants to be different', or indeed those people whose agendas will be to get the best deal for themselves. Actually, Britain risks to lose a lot if Article 50 is invoked.

There could be a fairly correct offer in regards to Britain's current strength. But no one is able to pick just where on the balance the offer will be. The scales of Europe could well become as costly as those of Shylock, The Merchant of Venice. Germany, for example could use their automotive strength to replace Britain's car export; France may possibly like to see British agriculture levied with a large tariff.

Lack of control on the terms wanted is a major factor of trying to avoid the Article 50 deal. This would allow the EU to cherry pick what suits them best. If they decide Britain is a hindrance to the EU goal of one union, it can then together insist through the deal that Britain must comply with their whims. This almost certainly would mean a reduction of Britain's current, rather nice, deals and quite simply it may, and can, and then Britain must accept or leave.

The most important point for a British referendum voter to remember is that whatever deal is offered must be aimed at bringing Britain together in an ever closer Union, which is something the British public are not keen on. The deal could even go so far as no more opting out, or the enforcement of the remaining ninety five or so points of the Lisbon Treaty. This would be a devastation for British economy. It would be the final demise for the Sterling, and the end to the European juggling act Britain has practiced since 1990 – the poisoned joining of the ERM which lasted just 2 years before Germany refused to help a friend and fellow European economy, a decision which turned the sides of several other countries ready to help.

European leaders could use the impending death of the Sterling as a subtle way to move out a lot of Britain's financial strength and GDP profit towards Europe. One lady once referred to it as a back door to one economic union. That lady stood strong against the political Europe while teetering with the financial aspect. She saw the Bank of England's interest rate rise from around 8 per cent in 1988 to 15 per cent in 1990; an increase at too greater rate to be sustained.

The deal, however Europe give it, must follow the Union's principle targets and therefore can be well summarised in the words of the aforementioned lady, Baroness Thatcher:

"The president of the commission (Jacques Delors) wanted the European parliament to be the democratic, the commission to be the executive and the council of ministers to be the senate"

Why do I say that the new deal could go very wrong for Britain? If a leave vote is achieved, the Mother of Parliaments has no more cards to play; Britain's hand is fully exposed while not one of Europe's cards have been shown. It could be the subtle excuse certain countries leaders have been hoping for to force Britain's hand, or push them out. If Britain votes to stay, Europe knows it has the control needed over Britain to refuse further opt out requests.

There is only so much positive data that Britain can wave in front of the EU for a better deal. Europe, like a pack of wolves standing in strength, could take to heart the words of Britain's very own Baird Shakespeare, celebrating the 400th anniversary of his death; by announcing the death of his home land.

"Be not afeard; the isle is full of noises."

People say the choice is leave or stay, but essentially Europe could reject Britain in favour of tailor made agreements best suited to themselves. Like a publican to Shakespeare, they could say: "get out, you're baird". The media having focused so much on Britain's decision has already successfully covered everyone's eyes of the long term and indirect third option: Britain united more to the dream of one economic and political union. The Eurosceptic party are too intent on pushing to leave, and Europe to a point does not want the British voter to consider what must happen if Britain stays; she must be more inclusive, more willing, more on board, ultimately, less British.

European Parliament has many self-appointed members, or friends invited to take place. It is like the fat geek in school who always got picked last in gym class then decides to start his own team just to have some authority. This is the sort of behaviour we see in frontier markets where political coups take place.

There may not be much positive publicity in Britain for the current President of the European commission, Jean-Claude Juncker. He was however a man leading a party with the majority vote but was forcedly ousted of his position by the evil scheming of the current *Premier*, Xavier Bettel - a two faced man whose dream since youth was to be Prime minister of Luxembourg, while publicly denying it. This, is the European way.

If Britain votes to leave or stay in the hope of better agreements, then she must wake up and smell the rain. The Central European mentality is not to give on what one warrants, but on ease of choice and simple division. If this is the way the deal be offered, the British will keep half of what is good for them and receive weakened offers on the other half, and as compensation be handed pittances in return. There may be deal changes for Britain, but even if 'better' is what she can ask, it is not what she shall receive.

Weaker economies within Europe will fight for better rights, just like Malta has already publicly stated, and larger economies will avoid as much as they can to stand for Britain's cause; no large economy will risk being the exception which sides with the rebel in a potential European split. The risk for the Islands is to receive embittered prejudice. For the voter, to leave and getting stuck in limbo is a bad fence-sitting decision which amounts to giving up on something so many other countries need. Voting to stay avoids the risk of a worse deal. But the damage has been done, the politicians upset, the world stirred, the bluff called. Britain must either become European, or get out and stay out.

This net importer cannot afford to overlook the dangers of backing out now. The anchor Baroness Thatcher tried so hard to place; the strong pound in a free market while reducing taxes through tightened government spending is in danger. Britain has grown quicker than most in Europe recently, but the twin deficit has gone from a few hundred million to well into three billion in just five years. All this is a sign of a weaker pound to come.

Whatever happens, Europe has Britain isolated on a negotiation table because Britain and France are the only large EU countries carrying debt levels expected from Emerging Markets. The only other EU countries carrying higher levels of debt are those slated for being almost bankrupt within the last six years.

Britain is not a commodity resource rich land to recover. Its commodity is now actually Services and these can be done freely without needing to suffer large Tariffs. If ever there is a time to get out, it is now. It is the only good opportunity that has presented itself in twenty four years. There was one opportunity in the past, however that would have caused instability. Now it offers the risk of the same, but this time with growth attached.

It is for the politicians to present facts and not preferences, so that the public can make an informed decision. Where are these politicians who can stand and be counted?

Occasionally I am asked whom I think is the best British prime minister that has ever lived. I blame my young years and the fact I moved away from the white cliffs with just twenty four years of age as the reason I cannot put a name to it. Instead, I believe that the great British Prime Ministers are the ones who look not to mock the opposition policy, but will instead only look to what Britain can offer to the world, and what it needs to do so. Only sorting its own problems while also looking to serve others can any country be well run.

I remember a tongue in cheek comment I once posed as a teenager to an old friend; a staunch Conservative who was intent on getting into politics. During one of his propaganda missions at our pub table, I question why the politicians are even there. After all, on the television all they do is mock or jest at another simply because of the person's party affiliation. They then occasionally discuss very trivial matters about one of their constituents, matters which could be sorted in a jiffy without the need of the time of so many people.

Essentially, the country could run itself with a skeleton parliament given that once the budget is allocated, councils are in place to spend it as needs may be - Belgium does not do too badly with their parliamentary set up...

In typical parliamentary fashion, my friend refused to answer but simply scoffed that I am not welcome to the conversation (I use the word 'conversation' in a rather liberal sense, as he was delivering what seemed much more like a dictation).

But in reality, politicians are there to do what is best for the nation. It is not limited to the needs of the current tax payers, nor is it limited to the people who receive their pensions now. It is not even limited to the next generation, but it is for long term stability. This is to ensure that economic factors such as investment, employment and trade, social factors such as education and health care and transport factors such as infrastructure are taken care of, relevant to the needs of the country.

I had gained a lot of respect for Cameron that in spite of his own opinion he was willing to do what the country wanted him to do; by bringing this historical moment to a referendum. But sorry, Cameron on his mission to convince Britain to stay in Europe claims Britain leaving would cause World War Three and mass genocide. Come on son. There is scaremongering and complete codswallop. World War Three is not far away given the global economy, given the tensions between massive countries, given one country's need to have every other march in step with the stars and stripes, given migration on vast scale, given the clashing of cultures, given the hatred we allow ourselves to breed for other humans, given the lack of value we put on the welfare of another being. Britain leaving would be just another small step of uncertainty.

What is he thinking, really? As if the bunch of islands called the United Kingdom floating in the pond will suddenly become a meek, vulnerable, and yet attractive island to own? And Europe, or a group of people would decide to make them their own? This is a plot a Johnny English Villain would come up with! What a fantastic way to lose any shred of respect yours truly was giving him.

Lost the plot is essentially how I can describe the Prime Minister at the moment. People thought the rugby tackling former London mayor Boris Johnson was a Looney, but at least he is showing some sense, and some facts, although he has made enough comments to be Britain's very own Donald Trump (minus the racist hints, of course). Up until now, the UK politicians for staying in Europe have only used manipulation, and quotes from Financial organisations, whom do not want the potential instability which may come as the result of the split.

Remember the IMF and ECB have a lot of money sitting on the Europe project working, especially Greece's shoulders. They have gone all in, and ignored their own regulations of risk management. If Britain leaves and it signals a walk out of certain countries, then the nearly bankrupt countries would be the first to jump. Greek voters have shown their opinion only too well that they do not want to pay back the country's debt. Italian banks have dropped approximately 50 per cent in share value in just the first four and half months of 2016. Spain is currently showing unemployment at approximately 20 per cent - a massive improvement since 2009 but it is still 20 per cent.

Another suggestion was that house prices will collapse? No, House companies will struggle, a lot. This is because there are many companies doing mass projects, and are relying on a continued increase of house prices above interest level; this is overstretching on their part. But this is no collapse. At worst there is a 4-8 per cent drop in real estate which can be factored in, but this is actually a positive given the difficulty for young couples and families to get on the Property Ladder. Even if the market takes a dip and the lenders, because of recent history knee jerk and become even more strict on giving mortgages - as a protection against the risk to their balance sheets which the break from Europe would bring - there would soon enough be an easing of lending policy and the chance to get a mortgage at low rates. If one is in the position of being able to re-mortgage his house in the event of a leave decision, then go for it once the initial dip has levelled out and laugh all the way back to the bank as the value corrects back up at a quicker rate than the interest will ask, and a better rate than most financial products would offer.

Britain's request for better terms was already rejected by EU. The offer the EU returned was not good. If Article 50 is triggered, a new deal will be offered a new deal by the rest of the EU, which will be final. Britain can leave, or accept the deal and then stay in Europe with that deal. Will the government even bring that choice to the public, or will they, like John Prescott simply take the decision upon himself?

Essentially, if a voter wants to leave, the vote option is obvious. If a person however just wants better deals, they need to accept it will not happen, but if they really want to try and get some better terms, he must by default vote to leave. The deal will not come without a majority leave vote. The only way to get renegotiated terms now is to vote to leave. But there is no guarantee the other European countries would give a better deal. We need to remember and be wary about the fact that Britain only pays about half of the membership cost compared to that of other European countries, and being an exception brings many problems, deserved or otherwise. Dealing with Europe is like card games in with a casino. Hope is for the hopeful before an event, yet reality is for the ones who lived the history, and a European deal could well be for a fool.

9 THE NEXT MOVE

An appeaser is one who feeds a crocodile hoping it will eat him last - Lechat

Trade negotiations are always interesting. While it is true that a certain level of promotion is needed, one does not need Jeremy Clarkson and Top Gear to travel the world to promote British products like they did on their India Road Trip. Britain has a legendary reputation for trading and has for a long period, since the British Empire in fact, been a country built on trading of goods. This has however slowed down in correlation with the raw material resources from its geographic region, and although the pound has remained strong, the purchasing of developing countries' resources has not been enough to sustain Britain's market share. Services requiring office space have really taken over as the government's main tax income.

Without this Importing, the strong currency is not as important as before. Although Britain should if possible avoid the currency weakening too much as it does reduce the spending power of households, businesses and the government.

Economic factors always change, but there is a way to ensure the trend is more favourable than otherwise. Germany moved from one of the worst performing European countries over the last two decades of the twentieth century, to one of the most stable of the last decade (yes, the eighties and nineties were no friend to Germany). Britain can do the same if it conducts and stands by structural reforms. Sure this can hurt, but being lean for a while can be more useful long term.

There is always the tempting route along the lines of the one which Portugal tried; ignore issues and simply join the single monetary currency... this helped them to turn an almost 15 per cent growth of

GDP per capita of a thirty year period into no actual growth. This is well and truly backed up by data showing that this wonderful achievement was done by procrastination and the taking of the Euro as its currency. Whatever decisions Britain and its politicians will make in the near future; I sincerely hope they are not like that!

Britain voting to stay would mean that she continues in the EU, as things currently are, however the sentiment I get is that Europeans hold a level of bitterness towards Britain. To stay is not just accepting to support the EU in its plan; but to walk in step with it. Can Britain afford to do this knowing the next five to ten years bring European economic struggles and a continued increase of Britain's twin deficit. Without Budget cut backs, there is no way for Britain to rein in those debt levels, especially as there is no actual growth forecast for Europe within the next three years.

Sure, there is artificial growth via loose monetary policy, but it does not bring strength. Just like an athlete can only be good if he is also mentally sharp as well as physically, an economy must not only have growth but it must be with strength. On the other hand, a way to keep the peace would be to vote to leave but make it clear we would be looking for a continued union in terms of trade, which would hopefully appease certain nations. The easiest would be to tell the European leaders that Britain is looking for a specific model, but here start the issues. No current model European trading model offers anything to Britain's strengths.

As with all EU countries, Britain is part of the EEA. There is the possibility of remaining in the EEA like Norway, Lichtenstein and Iceland, which are technically EFTA countries. Ironically these countries are expensive compared to most EU members. The risk for Britain is that being out of the EU, but still in the EEA means that certain regulations will be levied onto Britain without them having any control on the discussions and with no possibility to opt out; while still having no cessation of free labour movement.

The very things Britain needs to get on her side in the coming few years is the reduction in membership costs so that the twin deficit can be brought back in order without jeopardising trading costs, a grip on the levels of immigration and the control over their currency while an increasing export. Being in the EEA will not reduce membership costs, however it will permit the avoidance to bailout an EU country if needed, and finally there is no possibility of border control.

As only one of the four needs are met this way - the keeping of the Sterling - Britain would need some clauses set on this option. It will be extremely unlikely that Britain be either offered this or would take it. Britain's strong economy could allow at least a request for special limitations on labour and immigration laws, but then Norway does not have this and yet it holds the largest sovereign wealth fund in the world.

Britain could leave the EEA and return to being just part of the EFTA in a set up as Switzerland is currently engaged. Britain used to be a part of this, leaving in 1972 to join what is now the EU. This is generally more beneficial for a service based country, however for Britain in terms of export it becomes an expensive position, adding much more cost than the current set up with the EU. The UK is a net importer, and although the government would take less direct strain, the extra cost of living would put extra pressure on the households. Accepting either of these deals would risk this future inclusion into the Eurozone, that is, Britain denominated by the Euro.

There is also the Special Customs Union like Turkey has with the EU. This allows the free trade of goods; however, services are still eligible to tariffs. Given Britain's current revenue and net profit is service based, this would be a disaster and essentially the promise of all that is negative.

This leaves us with the very referendum option: Leave, and accept Standard WTO trading rights. This would create waves, not because it is essentially a catastrophic world changing event, because once the logistics are worked out the actual impact should be a much smaller impact than the media has been portraying it but because too many investors are on the markets with too much of other people's money. This deleveraging has already happened in preparation of the decision and the investment money is just sitting waiting to pounce, and pounce it will. The moment the decision is known, we will see short term market movement way more than they should as the rush to certain investments takes place. The movement of money away from the risk should displace markets by a few percent, but the leveraging of positions can mean sharp changes of anything up to 20 percent. This is not the fault of Britain, but rather the people living in the developed economies looking for extra gain on smaller market changes.

In the older English language, there are many French idioms that are thrown about. We have seen many times a déjà vu; will we see another? (cheap pun, I know). Soros smiles as he remembers Black Wednesday. What he 'achieved' back then was original and calculated, yet is now common trading practice. Short the market with borrowed money, and kill the opponent while he is down. In a generation which struggles with the concept of mercy and loves knock out sports such as MMA, it seems he was victorious. Sure, if riches are better than another's livelihood. Each one makes his bed.

What Britain is looking at is the need for new terms. Cameron has already tried and the results weren't great. If the vote is to leave, the terms thus likely proposed won't be any better.

While this may seem like there is no point even trying to get new terms, one must remember that a vote to stay is actually a vote to go with Europe, further into its existence, into its Union. There can always be a new vote in the coming years, but whether Conservative or Labour win the next election, it will not seem likely. The scary part is the vote to stay, and then the UKIP becoming at least part of a coalition at the next elections. That is the worst case scenario as the relationship with Europe would be insulted on a regular basis. The chances of a UKIP coalition with Britain staying in Europe is highly unlikely. It is nonetheless a risk, and one that will be worse even than voting to leave and then UKIP coming to power.

It is almost as if choosing to leave Europe means that the voting population would then automatically vote nationalist and the reason that certain politicians are touting this as a reason to stay. UKIP coming to power will not happen (he writes with angst); neither will it be that the other government parties would just disband if Britain is no longer in the EU. What does Britain do in its chessboard strategy? Does it have a real strategy, or is it just throwing Pawns forward hoping for a weakness in the EU frontline. Surely like a crocodile will consume its pray; Europe will check Britain, but will not call it mate. Wordsworth said it as such:

"What we need is not the will to believe, but the wish to find out"

10 SCOTLAND; THE HOME OF THE BRAVE

"It's all for nothing if you don't have your freedom" – Mel Gibson's William Wallace

America loves to quote the Bill of Rights, the French have strikes, the Spanish the siesta. Arthur Scargill helped Britain to be known for the unions. Britain, it seems however, has given in on those days; meetings around tables with tea has turned into balloting boxes, what with all these referendums and such.

First Scotland voted whether to leave the union that is Great Britain. Now Britain is to vote on their position within the European Union and Scotland will then possibly, scrub that, almost certainly referendum to disunite itself from the kingdom while at the same time will also need to decide about voting to be an independent nation, that is, run by Brussels...

For many Europeans, Scotland appears as nothing but a name. Many, refer to London as Great Britain, which is probably why they want that holiday location - Britain (London, that is) - to stay in Europe.

Scotland however has its very own culture, its own lifestyle, its own pride, and some of the most beautiful countryside to rival anywhere on the Island. If The Lord of the Rings were to be filmed anywhere outside New Zealand, then Scotland is the natural replacement although the Palm trees could spoil the background (yes, tropical trees in that cold, wet land).

They have not only a beautiful country for the eyes, but it spreads across as much land as England. They also boast a small population which reads as a positive in regards to figures such as the GDP per capita. None of these things however, bear well for the calculation of debt should Scotland achieve its own independence. No matter how a possible Scottish referendum would turn out; regardless of the currency they would take, the size of the debt which England would burden them with in comparison to their current GDP would soon make the eyes sore again.

Scotland for those who are not sure, does actually have quite a lot going for it. They are a country providing a lot of services, three quarters of their GDP in fact, and it is home to two financial centres; Glasgow and Edinburgh. They may not be New York or Paris in terms of size, geographic, demographic status or indeed in anyway, and they may not be as attractive as fund paradises such as the Cayman Islands, but they do have one thing going for them; the potential to grow should the independence come to pass. Plenty of cheap land, and a doorway to and through Europe can really change the dynamic of the country and add some excellent real estate to the books of global Financial Institutions.

Just as the English took away the Scot's identity back when Britain expanded north of England's border, it looks like England have subtly taken the Scottish financial identity already: The Royal Bank of Scotland is the largest 'Scottish' registered company in terms of revenue but it is actually owned by the HM Treasury...

Scotland, whose reputation among the British is that of the Dutch amongst their European counterparts can aim to tailor certain products to take business from London, given that a Scotland in Europe offers the Fund Passports to businesses which a Scotland less Britain, or independent London could not.

In looking to increase their financial institution base, the door would be open for a quick, easy and cheap route to gain wealth through tax and can very easily be done if the British Government does not get its act together in finding a sensible proposal to the European Fund Passport headache. The influx which Scotland could achieve would stand them in good stead to handle the debt which Britain (England, this would then read) would throw at them. The only real fear would be inflation which could only be managed if they had full control of a currency. It could be a case of becoming too successful too quickly but yet one thing is certain; they could plunder England as quickly as England has Scotland in the past.

But before everyone gets carried away and starts buying real estate hoping to get rich from Scotland's green gold, the countryside, it might be good to look at how a Scottish government can miss the opportunities right in front of their eyes because they are blinded by another type of gold; Black Gold. Yes, oil alone provides between 10 and 20 per cent of the tax generated for Scotland each year - the whole of the UK has a tax revenue from oil of around 1.5 per cent. This would be yet another reason to buy land now, creating a mini rush like the fracking fields of North Dakota has done in recent years.

Scotland, according to figures published believes it has over 500 billion pounds of Oil and Gas still left to exploit, although the British Geological

Survey states this income is much lower. Whichever calculation appears to be the closest to the truth (my guess would be the independent BGS, knowing government desire to manipulate for their own good any statistics they please, which are of course eventually just an extension of lies…), a large percentage of this is in central Scotland slap bang under some of that amazing countryside I have previously referred to, meaning that topography would make it an expensive source to tap. The real figure of useful Scottish oil I expect would be therefore around 30-40 Billion GBP at current oil prices, using 40 USD a barrel as a reference. Given their reputation for being tight-fisted (I can neither confirm nor deny this as actually true), Scotland would not want to lose any part of their land, not even some islands floating way off their coast randomly stranded between mainland Scotland and Norway. This is a problem because without the danger of environmentalist movements against potential fracking, the most accessible oil fields for Scotland are in the territory of the Island groups; Shetlands, Orkney and the Western Isles, with Shetland alone accounting for 20 per cent of British offshore oil reserves. All three of these island groups stand as a majority against an independent Scotland and also a majority for remaining British.

With their desire to stay in Britain, Cameron should be looking to get these islands on board before Scotland's expected second referendum. The Island's first referendum attempt was finally closed, as the Committee whom launched the petition accepted Scottish Government's points that there was not enough time to hold the referenda for the islands (Shetland, Orkney and Western Isles).

All this attempting to keep for oneself that of another could means this new love of balloting may even descend into a skirmish or two. Whatever happens, 'civil' could carry a liberal meaning as I am sure England will stand up for the Islands, or at least for the protection of oil reserves – something only expected of America. The question for the uncertain future can be found in the not very clear past:

Did England save the impoverished Scotland, or did Scotland come to England's rescue at a time when it was defending itself against an onslaught from Europe? Whichever way pre-1707 history be told; it can be retold three hundred years later. But that was then. Now it is a matter it time, and only   time   can   tell   what   may   be.

11 BRITAIN OUT OF EUROPE

"We only part to meet again" – Black Eyed Susan, John Gay

In Britain's history there have been bold citizens whom have stepped up to take the reins and lead. Are the British really as confident as they come across or is the average Brit hindered by a slight complex of holding back, afraid he is possibly not as good as the next man. Does this lack of confidence translate to a fear of voting to leave? The growing support for the leave camp does suggest boldness is returning as the average John Smith realises he is not the only Joe rocking the boat that is Britain.

Brits have always been a reserved folk and it is a quality I miss, as those around me in Luxembourg suffer from ill-disciplined children who are much more heard and seen than any English bairn of my generation. Even just yesterday I was reminded of this trait as I was sat with a friend who is an anecdotal raconteur of typical 'life in the day of' scenarios. This lady recounted the time purchasing a ticket for the opera 'Nabucco' and in general chit chat let the gentleman employed at the Royal Opera House know that she performed the very opera during her school days many moons ago. Following this up, she questioned if she could sing along with the bits she still remembered. The ghastly horror upon the gentleman's face as he slowly peered up was enough that even the driest, wooden human being would break down in hysterics. This is not how Belgium views the Opera apparently, and not how Europe views life.

Whatever it is in the mentality, be it that Britain is a series of Islands, or the sub-conscious thoughts being that little bit outside of Europe in geographical terms, British people do not feel European. In

50

writing this book, I have studied poll after poll, and have yet to find one in which more than 30 per cent of the voters stated they feel European. There is also a definite pessimism of a Brit to Europe; and there is good reason for this. After all, we have seen in history how easily Britain was left out to dry. Political snideness of certain governments (of course I would not mention any government in particular, so to avoid getting caught in scandals or political correctness, we will just give these governments the generic term 'French'...) would mean whatever Britain decides now, trading would be minimal.

If Britain were no longer strongly encouraged to trade at least certain amounts with other EU countries then goods which have over time become imported products can be re-domesticated, ensuring the negative impact of lost trade be covered. This re-domestication would surely have extra cost, but would avoid import charges if the finished products would otherwise be brought to the Islands. The outcome would be the cost of goods would remain similar to current values, while taxes paid would be for the British government. This gain would help to keep unemployment low, indirectly keeping the cost of living within control and inflation unaffected by the reduction of imported goods. Britain, calculated using GDP per capita is not an expensive area to live in, even so much that it can be considered cheap in comparison to other European countries.

This separation from the EU would allow skills lost to be re-groomed, and thus increase tax revenue without increasing costs. This has the end of reducing the current twin deficit and keeping control of the currency, and thus the sovereignty. How much will change in terms of immigration is yet completely open. Net migration is even harder to calculate until we know how many British will run away from its white cliffs should Britain leave.

Britain is currently one of the best performing developed economies in the world with over 2 per cent growth in GDP per annum. In Europe, only the developing markets and countries rebounding from devastating collapses currently post better results.

Economies take around six years following reform before the results are seen as solid continued growth. In six years Germany advanced through their Agenda 2010 campaign. In six years the US economy had already rebounded and recovered to stable levels equivalent of pre-Financial Crisis of 2008.

For Britain, who are now enjoying the period of reform by posting some of the most positive data in the developed world, the correcting of the remaining problems which they still have will allow continued growth into the next generation.

This done properly will be steady and positive. There is no need for guns blazing total reform, but at the same time Britain must make sure not to let up on its hindrances and must under no circumstances allow a political party from being voted in whose leader is a nationalist lunatic. Staying in Europe presents chances of EU subsidised projects. This is something Britain should be grateful for. Out of Europe, there is instead not only the chance but the need to reroute some of the money saved by leaving towards these projects, thus allowing a recirculation of the money as private firms employed in the projects would be able to pay more tax, and possibly more staff.

Unless Britain's issues are completely ignored, or managed completely wrongly, there is no long term down turn for Britain in choosing to leave. To avoid defending this statement with the placing of graphs all over the pages, I do not go into details about the statistics, knowing that the possible trade agreements with each country would mean the estimation contains an accumulated tolerance from many possible permutations. What is sure though is that an initial weakening of the currency due to the British deficits will allow for months of better export. If not to the EU, at least to other trade partners. This alone will help to stimulate business in the private sector and provide at least temporary jobs, which will absorb some potential job losses from multinational organisations which choose to leave. This referendum is the best chance for Britain to escape unscathed from a Union which is has been shy to for over sixty years. Avoiding Europe is not just an elder person disease of not wanting to change things they are, as the next generation still do not stand for being European because fundamentally it encroaches on being British.

I saw an article claiming that Britain is to flourish if it leaves Europe. This of course was the 'Vote Leave' Chief Executive Matthew Elliot who was interviewed for this. So a small reality check - something Europe believes all British people need - Britain is in no state to flourish. It does not have the capabilities, it's currency is already weakened and ready to weaken further and the Kingdom will suffer from reduced GDP per capita and a reduced tax purse while not being able to reduce the immigration to lower than 60,000; all pressures to cause a recession. It has too little in terms of modern infrastructure, and domestic trading. While Britain has more than enough skills and knowledge in certain sectors, she lacks the basics needed to provide long term stability and has imported too much in terms of goods for too long.

The Financial Times published an article supporting the other side of the debate, in which an apparent senior German politician stated that Brexit would be a disaster for Britain and a catastrophe for

Germany. While this makes sense, given that Germany has a positive Trade balance with the UK of over 50 billion Euro, that is 1.6 per cent of German GDP, I question if it really becomes an issue?

Well, not really. Just because Britain leaves, does not mean that Germany and Britain would give up on the relationship. After all, a separation from Europe does not mean end of all trading. Where the costs would go up, the governments can look for a trade agreement to set aside and dilute the effect of the costs; it is not as if the areas of trade are complete unknowns. We need to ensure we look at this sensibly.

Leaving Europe does not mean the end of all trading is imminent. Where both parties benefit, it would take a crazy government to avoid looking for ways to cushion the blow. Not many of Britain's big trading parties are run by such nationalists who would be willing to cut their noses off to spite their faces, except for those nations we are calling in this chapter 'French'. Europe however, have the right to block any country to country negotiations, meaning any Free Trade agreements would be ruled out unless done with the whole EU. Like a bully who will only let you play with his football if he can be captain, Europe will throw its weight around however it can to ensure the nimble striker Britain does not get chance to score.

Britain certainly does not have a party in power at the moment who would be looking to do destroy relations, or negotiate bad terms. In addition, Cameron is for Britain being in Europe so he will do his best to protect ties. Even if by the next election Labour find themselves in power, they have made it clear they not only see the future of Britain in Europe, but a move to take the Euro would be imminent, although not immediate. Essentially then, very little will change in how Britain and Europe do business. This then refers the referendum to its base which has been blinded by single factors and media spin: Does Britain want to be part of Europe's long term objective? If not, then staying a little longer is a recipe for disaster.

"There is a tide in the affairs of men, which taken at the flood leads to fortune…on such a full sea are now afloat. And we must take the current when it serves, or lose our ventures." – Brutus in Julius Caesar

If no trade agreement can be found between Britain and its biggest importers of British goods, it would take time for these countries to research and develop goods of the same quality at a competitive price, especially since the Pound would also be on a weakening trend. In terms of British imports, admittedly, we do risk losing certain French cheeses from the supermarket shelves. British transport logistics do risk lorries being blocked more and more at the French border. Something that I can confirm does not happen just at the border with Britain, however it is something Britain will suffer for generations to come as long as the average French mentality carries a political spite towards its island neighbours.

Just this weekend I entered into a pleasant yet brief conversation with a Scottish couple in a little Luxembourg village on the outskirts of the capital. The gentleman, a recently retired Health and Safety Inspector for a Scottish council and his better half, informed me that their European road trip suffered a diversion as there was no fuel to be found in France due to strikes. The gentleman also went on to mention that after visiting Greece so often as a tourist, he arrived in 2010 and was shocked at the apparent wealth of the nation and he said to himself "how on earth can Greece afford to live like this?" It was a thought he had only once more, when he arrived in Luxembourg in 2016. Quite simply, Greece couldn't.

Britain, unlike Greece, has not set itself up to live off free European money. Therefore, even with the current pressure on the developed economies, and the stress experienced by smaller or underdeveloped economies, Britain can accept the weakening now caused by leaving, so as to continue its aim of becoming one of the strongest economies in the future. Britain has an economy which can afford to weaken without jeopardising the quality of life. And in this lies one of the keys to the referendum:

Britain will suffer if it leaves, but it will suffer less than staying.

In the 2012 film Argo, a CIA Operative is brought in to consult on an operation to rescue some Embassy workers hiding out in the Canadian Ambassador's residence during the Iraq Embassy siege of 1979. In presenting an idea to create a fake science fiction movie so that the escapees can be smuggled out of the country as film crew, Ben Affleck playing the CIA Operative tells the Director of Central Intelligence:

"There are only bad options, it's about finding the best one."

The Director counters with:

"you don't have a better bad idea than this?"

The Operative's colleague's response comes:

"This is the best bad idea we have sir, by far."

Britain should no longer be debating if she should leave, knowing that she is bound for many years by the ensuing trade negotiations to replace the EU agreements. Britain should therefore be focusing on how she can manage growth through education, population, accommodation, business support and entrepreneurial aids. Because whatever the outcome of the vote, the issue is how the country is run. Now both the public and political focus is close to the topic, the government should be looking to address these issues. In fact, that is what Britain should be doing anyway because if the vote is to stay, then Brexit would have been much ado about nothing without anything being learnt. In Argo, Karl Marx is wrongly paraphrased, and what better way to address Brexit:

"History starts as a farce, and ends as a tragedy"

12 SUFFER, SURVIVE OR THRIVE

"Let us learn from the past to profit by the present, and from the present, to live better in the future" – Wordsworth

Now to Willy Wordsworth's wise words, Britain's ears should be open to hear, and the mind to listen.

The scene is set; Europe has an objective, an aim to head towards. The dream for Europe started small – grouping together certain resources - and has since grown by way of geographic inclusion. That small Coal and Steel project has since opened up many more areas to trade and union with the end objective of an 'ever closer union'. The end, logically, cannot come until the union is one, perfectly one.

It has that much needed direction but not everyone wants to tug towards *that* final point. Britain - for those fearing it - is not the only black sheep.

Britain was an early arrival and used Europe as the stepping stone to continued growth. One can only gesticulate through signs of the times if it really helped the Islands to be anchored to the mainland, although in the long term Britain has continued to be a major economy so it would be a bold claim to say it suffered more than it grew.

Not alone was this isolated island in becoming part of Europe in order to grow; most countries chose Europe at any given time in their history for their own good - those isolated geographically, and those politically isolated such as Croatia - causing the tailor made Europe origins to become generic. There are many countries, given the chance would at some point in their future say to Europe; "well I must be off now, nice to have known you and toodaloo".

Europe, and also the world, is slowing down. This does not seem logical, after all if somewhere slows down another place must speed up, surely, somewhere must be growing? But the phenomenon actually is about the recycling of money. Simply put if the money does not keep turning through trade and charges, then there is no distribution of wealth and no taxes on the distribution thus the slowdown happens. This decreases global government and central bank wealth, drawing down the economy which panics people to not spend, slowing the cycle even further. In addition to this, a lot of financial markets - which work off the data it sees - use money belonging to others, either via leveraging or wealth management. When things slow down, investors become reluctant, meaning less to invest and also less opportunities to invest in. The general growth of the last few generations has been because of the opening of the financial markets to public, in one form or another. Slowdown was inevitable and now countries which are not locked into expensive generic trading programs can be astute to make the best of what they can.

2007 and the USA went 'pop'; the world went 'yikes'. The markets naturally grew again as people chose an appetite for riches and making more money to whatever level of risk their stomachs could handle. The investor eventually looked to emerging markets in these better times and the beneficiary countries either have emerged, or fallen back because of their bad habits. The Frontier world continues with each country at its own random pace as would be expected from small economies with minimal regulation and remnants of corrupt political systems; be it families holding office, or positions of political power found by force.

The positive frontier economies, have learnt from the development achievements and mistakes of the countries which have gone before them. Expensive manufacturing is no longer the case because expensive trial and error projects are not needed in these countries; the old production lines from the developed countries are simply bought in. This contributes to a lack of spending and resource usage.

China and India were the last real hoorahs for a developing country trying to do it their way, backed by western money. So what happened when 'China went bang'? The world went 'ouch'. Only until recently has money moved back to investments in Emerging, Asian or Frontier markets, and again this is really only because people choose wealth instead of risk. A little European instability this June will just be enough to rock those investments gently on the waves and those investors with readily sea sick stomachs will let their risk aversion lead them to disinvest as soon as possible. Another piece of misery these countries are just hoping to go through...

Thankfully the sun rises in the east, and the short term hit these economies may suffer, may prove beneficial through FTA agreements with Europe and Britain separately, whatever their needs may be. This is the bespoke trade agreements needed in a time of global economic austerity. If Britain does boom, an export rich country such as Thailand can enjoy the extra business in electrical goods that the extra British household cash would buy. The car manufacturers in Britain can then smile as more units will move. This would be a nice pick-me-up to the economy and one that could sustain healthy figures. The recycling of money could then start up again. But only if Britain boom...A Britain in panic would slow the recycling and could equal a Britain bust. Like hitting 22 in a game of blackjack; its close, but no cigar.

Europe, whatever the British referendum decision, can only look to within for growth. Its aim to protect each country against a recession because of the free and encouraged trading between its countries is an oxymoron amongst the best. If any part of its union has a stumble and things go wrong, the union is called to move together...however this does not always happen.

Britain failed the ERM and were failed by the EU. Greece failed everybody and were supported to no end by Europe and even the IMF. Finland just afterwards chose self-inflicted austerity. Not because they were already in danger, but they helped themselves to avoid potential issues later. I think we all know Finland would not have been such as generous charity case for Europe as Greece continues to be. It is hard to see as of yet who will be the winner in all this Union stuff, but it is clear that among equals some appear more equal, while others are left outside the gates warming themselves around the Brazier.

As recent as these financial market crashes are, they are nonetheless the *past* which sets us now in the *present*. Britain *has profited from the Union* not so much in exporting goods but in opened doors to provide services. It was not Britain's original aim, but when Europe pulled, it was in a direction Britain could afford to go. Now, however, the islands must *profit from this present* and to do that must decide its direction and then take the necessary decisions, because only by knowing where one wants to be, can one head towards it. Each voter, regardless of his own preference should look at where he wants Britain to go in the future generations and decide if it can handle what it needs to do in this generation. Like a new born baby's father, he must take the decision to live for the family, not for himself. He must invest all that he is so that the baby does not want for life's necessities – anything else is annihilation.

Voting to stay is a vote to limit potential growth, but in spite of this negative, a stay vote potentially cushions any harsh domestic time Britain may find itself in. Like a Visa card insurance which is paid every month in the protection of the difficult times, Britain can keep its current ties for that safety. The visa card insurance is more often than not never needed. Britain cannot, without good reason, simply throw away this insurance style relationship all willy nilly relying on the economy to continue strongly, because a reduced international trade income means any trouble Britain may get into in the future can be much costlier due to a reduced GDP and a weaker currency.

A vote to leave would open up Britain to unknown volatility of trade discussions. The only sensible way to calculate this is to look at the average and the worst case scenario for each industry sector with every country, or at least current EU countries and then calculate the potential cost. The calculations need to include if that industry were to become a major revenue for Britain, or a 100 per cent import if needed. It also would need to be calculated with each country as they currently are, and then where each of them should be mid and long term. As you can imagine, the time needed to calculate this alone would take the rest of my career, by which time the data would be outdated and I would need to start again. I therefore would like to say that I took the time to check all of these figures and calculated them with complex formulae, but quite simply, I haven't.

I have however done some basic calculations in regards to certain markets which Britain needs for its own survival, and I am no longer worried; neither of the mid nor the long term impact of a British decision to leave.

I am actually now more concerned of the decision to stay, or worse; voting to leave but then accepting a deal to stay. I say this because what I have calculated shows the biggest economical risk on the globe for the next eight years is that of the near and middle east, and also the EU – primarily the developed Eurozone countries. Ok, I admit, just who can we trust to enter into new trade talks on Britain's behalf, and who can then run the country is actually quite a worry...the main worry, actually.

Hypothetically, Britain can stand its ground off the shore of France having an export level decreased by 5 per cent, also import being decreased by 5 per cent, all the while suffering raises relational to 5 per cent of current tariffs, which are all sensible outcomes, but she would still not see less than a 2 per cent Real GDP drop in her first full year outside of the EU. The Eurozone is realistically forecast at no more than a non-central bank manufactured growth of more than 1 per cent. However, and here it comes; the following two years should see British GDP advancing whereas the Eurozone will stagnate unless the ECB stimulates the economy again, thus overinflating Europe on false data, disallowing a stronger euro and thus keeping Europe's debt levels in USD at the same rate as now. Only the Financial institutions giving up on London and then migrating to Europe (or possibly Scotland) can the forecast for Britain be worse than these figures.

Do Financial companies then refuse to be based in Britain if the Brexit occurs? There is the expected loss of the European Fund Passport - a passport which allows certain Investment types to be marketed across country borders. This has people concerned that Financial institutions will therefore move from London to mainland Europe. Really? Is this as dramatic as people make out? Is there no way to find a solution in regards to the Fund Passport? Because last time I looked Switzerland had a healthy banking sector. There of course may be companies which relocate certain offices or branches and thus jobs, however most companies would not throw the baby out with the bath water; especially since a GBP denominated base diversifies risk as well as allowing for innovative products. Let us not forget that the UK offers some of the largest trading in the world in regards to Foreign Exchange, which alone is a multi-trillion-dollar business. Switzerland, that country land locked by Europe in the hills has its own currency, its own rules, its own financial products, yet still holds eligibility to passport mutual funds.

Manufacturers which use British parts will have to invest into research and development if they want to replace the quality of British products with an alternative European product. Would for example German automakers which are known for (albeit no longer worthy of) their reliability, look to replace some of the British made parts?

Would a company such as BMW compromise their position as number one car maker by changing suppliers away from a British supplier to a European supplier? My guess, if the professionalism of the staff at the BMW museum in Munich is anything to go by, the answer would be no. On one of my recent visits to Munich, I was awaiting the arrival of my brother at the museum when I was informed that it would be closing early for a special event and therefore if I wanted to visit I would need to enter in the coming minutes. I politely informed the gentleman that I would not like to visit, however I am doing so that my brother can be happy. I, in typical British fashion, tried just a little to wind him up by pointing out that BMWs are now boring, overrated cars which develop electrical issues that almost always strand the driver, and that to spend time looking at them was akin to sticking needles in my eyes (although the museum features only the old cars, which I actually do really like, as in, really like). The gentleman remained utterly professional, as he listened to my points and then countered ever so politely with 'as you wish sir'. Touché.

This professionalism is as expected from most of Europe that they will continue trading with Britain; it makes good economic sense and is of much more value than petty refusals to trade because of spite. An upset to all this would be more likely if Britain chooses to repeal the 1972 European Communities Act instead of invoking article 50. But even if Europe is really upset with Britain, once it finds itself in hot water, needing all of the help and trade it can get, it may just come knocking at the English Channel like a supranational Oliver Twist "Please sir, can I have some more?". But in reality, that is just not going to happen.

Britain leaving however will mean that the effects be felt throughout Europe. There is that apprehension that Europe is a supranational economy which is 'too big to fail', but maybe actually it is 'not small enough to be succeed'. Just as America does well, certain states are in decline. Or Russia, who rely on much less than half of their geographic area for 99 per cent of their GDP, Europe can also have its own Narnia – a place so different to the rest, that it be trapped in winter by the reign of the wicked Queen whom we call Europe. It is easy now to say that cannot happen - Ukraine may say it differently - so it is best to remember that even between trading parties, some get squeezed out. I mentioned Venezuela and OPEC earlier; they are a prime example of how being a part of something brings only suffering. The economic situation in Venezuela is now so bad that Coca Cola have given up on the country.

Some companies such as BMW have gone on record to say they will leave England's green and pleasant land. This threat of unemployment has been used to position their employees to vote as is the wish of company directors - directors that mostly sit in a German residence. This is a shame that some of these who are not entitled to vote choose rather to meddle in British minds on the topic. Of course a business needs to analyse its positives and negatives, but the vote is much more than just a vote of best trade value; the whole livelihood of Britain is on the line, the affiliation one has with its country, the education system it puts in place, how a worker is recompensed, how justice is done are all factors that a Brit needs to consider. For a European to reduce this vote through mental war play is a travesty of human rights – something Europe claims to stand for. This, is the European way.

Britain leaving would eventually risk jobs at certain companies, which the ensuing unemployment rate increases would allow other companies to have a better choice of whom to employ, therefore can decrease cost to the end of creating greater company profit. Taxes are then paid on the extra profit, replacing some of the taxes lost via factory and plant closures. Handled correctly by the government and councils, job losses have a knock on effect which lead to competitive prices and more employment. The government must be prepared to accept and help the certain towns which will be worst hit, knowing that certain local councils would undergo a sudden increase in the local unemployment. But then, we may just get more British comedy films like The Full Monty…

Britain provides a lot of services and long term these will enable money to come into Britain, which will help in controlling to an extent the monetary policy. Also a strengthening of the Pound once the market has corrected will allow cheaper imports and indirectly improve government spending. The share prices of the floated companies would return to fair value. The SME companies which avoid bankruptcy during the first couple of years will return to where they are around now, with some exceptions being at a stronger level than they were in 2015.

The issue we must not overlook is the customs tax which may then be levied. Service based companies run risks in this category, especially if they have outsourced certain tasks to EU countries which then are unable to achieve certain trade agreements. This would increase cost to the end user, and would be a negative notch for inflation. This could also be a negative factor for services provided by the UK to other European countries, as the lack of control and impending uncertainty over British monetary policy would make business investment opportunities riskier than most would like.

Britain would have to pay tariffs for items sold to the EU. Agriculture would be a big hit, as the typical tariff applied to EU imported products is close to the 50 per cent mark. That means for Britain to secure an average trade deal with the EU, every pound of a product would eventually have a value of 1.50 pounds. This will destroy its competitive edge, no matter how much the Europeans love the British cuisine…

An example is that in spite of the French protesting against British Beef, 90 per cent of all UK Beef exported goes to the EU. While this in terms of GDP is not a huge amount, the cost of Beef in Europe would increase too much to hold any real value, risking the livelihood of cattle farmers. Even the Aberdeen Angus would no longer appear as the special Beef on the restaurant menu. This massive drop in demand would hammer down the domestic prices - which is usually a good thing for a consumer - but we need to remember that if Britain as a country chooses to leave, it should look to support its workers, especially those who supply the food to our tables. We will see farmers, who already look to diversify their income will have to find more ways to support themselves and their families. As the amount of cattle needed would decrease, one option could be that the government offer to buy part of a cattle farmer's land for development.

German automotive industry stands to lose and gain, and as a result is one of the markets open to the most upset. The amount of German cars brought to Britain represents more than 50 per cent of Germany's total export to Britain. Interestingly, from the other side, more than half of the cars exported by Britain are imported by Europe. A typical tariff of 10 per cent on these cars can be just enough that it is almost as cheap to turn to BMW for one of their unoriginal and uninspiring entry level cars instead of that of a 'lesser brand' built in Britain.

Britain will almost certainly charge tariffs on EU imports, thus pushing up prices and inflation. The offset of a decrease in net migrants would not be enough increase wages enough to cover inflation. This is the basis of the IMF's concerns, and the facts and figures that Cameron as Prime Minister is using to scare people into a 'stay' vote.

Another issue is the level of Foreign Direct investment in the UK. While a lot of money is held in portfolios based through London companies, there is a much greater amount of money invested because of international companies whose plants and factories exist to supply the UK and even the world. The good news is that while these are at risk, the plants supplying only the UK will not close down; Britain is not in an unstable situation such as Venezuela, where it is better to jump than sit waiting for the bomb to explode. To protect the companies from selling, the natural risk to the stock market price would ensure the owners think twice about selling so much market share in one go, unless a buyout takes place. This FDI is therefore actually protected. But, and here this word becomes one of the biggest in the dictionary: Approximately 30 per cent of this FDI is into Financial Services. These services provide access to decentralised markets and therefore can be marketed from many places in the world.

There is no protection for Britain against the massive banks shutting their doors and selling off their shiny real estate, real estate which is so readily seen across London's financial region and has for many years now depicted London as a world class Financial Centre.

Britain is not ahead of Europe in terms of regulation, in fact, a European would describe Britain as being behind. I would like to say that the British use more common sense and it is a reflection of the difference in mentality of mainland Europeans and the little islanders. But for better or worse, a European mentality would prefer the regulations and thus a company such as Deutsche Bank could easily decide to close their business in the UK. It would be a bold move, but if it were to take place from a big name, this unrest will ripple along the Thames to those close by and would hurt tax income, a lot. This sector alone is a yearly profit of 16 billion pounds for the UK, which works out to a lot of pennies!

Put into perspective with the rest of British figures, the UK contributes 18 billion pounds to the EU Budget. Which when netted with returns means Britain contributes 10.5 billion. Europe does give back a couple of billion to business, and although this money is not counted because it does not pass between the central banks, a cool net 8 billion pounds is still going towards Europe. A Peter Kay style shop worker would have a great time counting out that amount into one's hand.

Knowing the facts can allow a Brit to make an informed decision, and also the boldness to stand by what he chooses. But if he chooses to leave, he chooses to let a new person run the country. Does such a person capable of taking the reins really exist, or will Britain be waiting for Santa Claus to fly in and deal with the present?

"England expects that every man will do his duty"
– Lord Admiral Nelson

NORMAN B. LECHAT

INVESTOR'S ANNEXE

Gambling, such a dirty word amongst many western cultures. Investing, quite the opposite. So what is the difference? Simply exchanging the words 'odds' for 'alpha' and 'strategy' for 'beta' can be sufficient. But one difference I see and live on is that sometimes, just sometimes, investments are clearly going to be winners. So obvious in fact, that it is child's play. I guess that is why so much active monetary policy goes on amongst western countries.

The last years have seen QE in an attempt to avoid recessions and all it has done is overinflate the markets and to some point set up a whole string of artificial figures which are still manipulated using old models.

I am not a fan of active monetary policy (if I had not made that clear...) as it distorts the reality and confuses the models which are based on predefined factors. I believe that as long as the economy has floating markets, one should accept the existence of fluctuations without meddling, only getting involved when the need is really there. It seems as though these last years, Central Bank leaders have had a need to prove they are the clever ones in the class, and thus constantly try to manipulate the economy every time there is a slight trough on a graph. Not very much of this has worked because it does not take investors long to spot the moves. Mario Draghi may start his speeches with such bold words as:

"This shows the monetary policy is working"

But essentially it just showed an over interest in a chart reflecting manipulated markets at the neglect of the real market situation.

At the beginning of this year I opened my third private fund, with the intro stating the following.:

"We stand on the edge of some of the most historical turbulence the financial markets have seen and 2016 will open and go down in history as a period of corrections, twitches and panics. To this end, I offer a cumulative 5 per cent a month gross growth of each portfolio for each of the opening three months".

There was no large hedging done, no need to borrow huge amounts to achieve this promise. The second global stock market correction in six months was previewed, the oil price war clear, the panic rush to gold foreseen, the migrant movement toward Europe putting strain on the larger European economies, and the potential Britain Europe split able to shake the currencies a few percent. Mix all of this with historically low interest rates, continued active monetary meddling, sorry, policies, and Japan a safe haven having no monetary policy protection and it was a period I was only looking forward to. Currently myself and my clients are enjoying this period, and without having to go for the jugular of any country or political movement.

An example of an easy trade in recent years was on Greek Bonds. Those of us who could, took the time to enjoy the short term yields on the Greek bonds, knowing Europe would stand by and protect a member country at least once – if not for unity, then at least in fear of the unknown to avoid the crumbling of the monetary union. Will Europe's fear of the unknown be an advantage to Britain this time around?

The hinging factor for investments short and mid-term due to the whole debate, referendum and impending changes - regardless of the eventual referendum decision - is the value of the pound, and what its true value means for investors dependent upon their domiciliation and base currency. Stocks are dependent of it; bonds are useless if the currency value drops; and assets are only good if they hold a value increasing at a rate at least equivalent of interest.

Just as banks try to hedge risk by diversifying across currencies, British retail investors (the average homeowner with a portfolio of investments alongside a pension plan) should have been doing the same as the media attention of Brexit increased. This is the first step in managing a portfolio for households whose base currency is the Great British Pound.

Traders who have done this have already seen nice gains as the pound has weakened, and hopefully already took the opportunity to profit from Gold bought against GBP – the natural next step as uncertainty increased. Markets remain on edge as the leverage has disappeared. Those in the know have their options in place to cover whatever outcome and profit from the eventual market moves. Now it is time for step three.

For investors who have not yet hedged across several currencies, it is too late to start this strategy as the pound risks rebounding in the summer of 2016. Instead, they need to move straight to step three.

The month of June 2016 will see continued deleveraging of GBP holdings, which will, like a spring pushed together allow a recoil once the referendum is over. There are many futures contracts already taken for settlement in July. The financial institutions and other professional investors will take these and expect a nice pay out for their hedge funds, balance sheets and general bonuses. What we will see is the opportunist jumping on the bandwagon as the Pound starts to move one direction. Day traders will have a field day, especially if the vote is to leave. Whatever the decision, it will push the Pound past its true value. This will be the time to move. But which way?

If the referendum votes to stay, we will see the pound strengthening. We will see the Euro strengthening. We will see the USD, Swiss Franc and Japanese Yen all weaken. Gold in GBP will drop harder than any other commodity. Those who are confident enough to trade Gold, and have a good enough Platform to do so, can hedge the risk by short selling Gold against the Pound, and by buying a smaller value of gold against the US Dollar. This will really dampen profits, but will protect the portfolio in case of adverse reactions. This of course is the plan if one does not know how to trade futures contracts.

There is always the counter risk that even a vote to stay will cause other European countries to rise up and demand better deals within Europe. As mentioned earlier, several countries have stated their intention for better terms. Because of this, the majority of investments should be done with some hedging, either through hedged transactions, or contracts.

The British and European stock markets will see money returning but not great amounts. The FTSE100, which because of the size of the companies listed is viewed as the safest and most stable of the British stock markets will see the money come back first, but really only gently. Both currencies are currently weak, with the Sterling index even below 85. This weakness is good for those who can get in now and use the regained pound strength to capitalise. But one needs to be wary because as the Pound will increase, so the cost of stocks will become less attractive. This means that the time to purchase shares of FTSE100 companies is now, but only providing Britain choose to stay. Those who can and know how to take contracts should be looking to buy before the referendum, with an option for July. This will be the protection should the vote be to leave and the market subsequently drops.

The British stock markets are a sensible investment should

Britain choose to leave because the weakening Pound will allow a cheaper share price. A note is to make sure that the companies to choose be mainly domesticated trade and carrying low debt liabilities. If one wants to long the market, it should only be done once the pound weakness levels out, as seen by the charts of GBP against the other reserve currencies.

So if the vote is to leave, the most foresighted trade of the previous few years is the shorting of the pound against other reserve currencies, although one should pay attention to the strength of the Yen and the possible Europe downturn which could touch a finance based economy such as Switzerland. I personally look to long USD and NOK (Norwegian Krone). I believe a smarter move is to take gold against the Pound. For the conservative portfolio, I would let the Euro weaken a little on the result, and then look to 3-year Euro bonds. Thanks to Britain's level of debt, the value of the pound is essentially being propped up by Britain's link to Europe and leaving will hammer this down. The housing market on the other hand, which naturally factors continued demand would at worst be only just propped up if Britain tries to close its borders, or alternatively could have a rally as land becomes cheaper and the Bank of England has to hold off on interest rate hikes in spite of a weakening Pound.

This land price does not rely only on a growing population, rather the other two factors previously mentioned are the ones to watch if real estate is an interesting investment opportunity for you. Landlords however need to be aware as the change in British law to tax landlords on the value of the property rather than the income may make a potential windfall into a constant headache.

If the population rate continues being higher than GDP growth, then a recession is on its way. Recessions are not actually so bad, as long as they are not long term. Britain has no way to reduce its governmental costs as long as it remains in Europe, other than to reduce trade which is then counterintuitive in clearing the twin deficit. Essentially, Britain needs to start being a nett exporter, but also export less total value than now just to avoid the extra costs. A slightly weakened currency and a continued emphasis on services is the most cost efficient way to do this. Does leaving Europe bring all the answers though? If only it were that simple...

For stock market traders in the event of a leave vote, thanks to the taxes applied to assets/liabilities for EU countries in regards to UK international assets, we are looking at a chance of EU money flowing out of the UK companies. This is both from the lending (liabilities) and the return (assets). This would push down the holding of business, but ultimately just through the rebalancing of the books causing a draw down on spending power which would in turn draw down the stock price as the P/E ratio would drop significantly. The stock would then be set for a bull as it would be better rated to other companies in the same sector, all the while the currency would also strengthen as confidence in the UK returns, pushing the stock position farther into profit.

The SME sector can see some mild growth for companies whom provide possible investment opportunities to long only strategy Funds. The UK Mid cap market stands to benefit the most, however the pressure in the small cap sector, with an increased level of bankruptcies will be something to avoid.

UK has been disinvesting its FDI in Europe these last years - over 20 billion GBP per annum – which leaves very little British FDI in Europe, whereas the EU still holds many billions in the UK; actually over 50 per cent of the FDI in Britain comes from EU. This is a worrying figure and one which means that the Large cap sector will have a good shake up as the international companies in Britain will see downward pressure, while the domesticated companies can already see light at the end of the Brexit tunnel.

If Britain does leave, it will just be another blip on the global financial markets creating further pressure on emerging and frontier markets to default. Most of these markets continue to lose currency value against the dollar, for which most of its debt is based and any uncertainty will further strengthen the dollar.

Life is divided into three terms – that which was, which is, and will be. Where does Brexit figure in your plans?

Brexit (adj.) a term used to describe the almost European exit of the small but once Great Britain. It was taken with the presupposition they were at the time actually in it.

THE MAN THAT IS:

Norman B. Lechat is one of the pen names used by this English Entrepreneur settled in Luxembourg. Hailing from Middlesbrough in the North East of England, he is qualified in Analytical Chemistry, Physiology and Financial Analytics. Lechat runs Private Wealth Investment Funds alongside his Production company. He has written several Film Scripts under another pen name. But this, his third book is the one that helped him realise his mortality as a mystery illness struck him down, affecting his lungs and heart.

Currently setting up a Health Centre, a series of recreational companies and being a minor partner in a Mobile Phone Application, Lechat is still found at all hours connected to his work.

"Holidays are a thing of the past, and a dream of the future. I have sacrificed what people spend their lives searching for so that I can provide the entertainment for their lives. Time has caught up with me but until the sand stops flowing, I am going to keep on running" he states when asked how he manages to keep so many projects going.